STEELTOWN BLUES

A NOVEL BY
RICHARD E. MOUSSEAU

MOOSE HIDE BOOKS
imprint of
**MOOSE ENTERPRISE PUBLISHING
PRINCE TOWNSHIP
ONTARIO, CANADA**

Cover illustration by Richard Mousseau

STEELTOWN BLUES
BY
Richard Mousseau
Copyright July 17, 1998

Published December 1, 1998
By
MOOSE HIDE BOOKS
imprint of
MOOSE ENTERPRISE PUBLISHING
684 WALLS ROAD
PRINCE TOWNSHIP
ONATRIO, CANADA
P6A 6K4
Web site www.moosehidebooks.com

NO ADVENTURE UNATTAINABLE

THIS BOOK IS A WORK OF FICTION. NAMES, CHARACTERS, PLACES AND INCIDENTS ARE EITHER PRODUCTS OF THE AUTHOR'S IMAGINATION OR ARE USED FICTITIOUSLY. ANY RESEMBLANCE TO ACTUAL EVENTS OR LOCALES OR PERSONS, LIVING OR DEAD, IS ENTIRELY COINCIDENTAL.

ALL RIGHTS RESERVED, NO PART OF THIS BOOK MAY BE REPRODUCED, THIS INCLUDES IN RETRIEVAL SYSTEM OR TRANSMITTED IN ANY FORM BY ELECTRONIC MEANS, MECHANICAL, PHOTOCOPYING, RECORDING OR OTHER, WITHOUT WRITTEN PERMISSION FROM THIS PUBLISHER.

CREATED IN CANADA

Library and Archives Canada Cataloguing in Publication

Mousseau, Richard E., author
    Steeltown blues / Richard Mousseau

ISBN 978-0-968185-28-5 (PBK).,--ISBN 978-1-927393-43-7 (PDF)

    I. TITLE

PS8576.0977S75 1998   C813'.54   C98-900905-X
PR9199.3.M675S75 1998
PS8576.O977S75 2017   C813;.54   C2017-901664-4

STEELTOWN BLUES

CHAPTER 1
MEMORIES IN A SONG

Again, the sounds of relentless pain, then there was a silence in the air. Cool wet mud soothed a still face as it slowly sank into the earth. All of the events over the past couple of months, even the past year, seemed forgotten. A mouse, small and innocent wandered through the tall green grass. Boo wondered if it was able to get away from the pursuers. A reflecting headlight from a distant Jeep glimmered against the far evergreen trees.

"Do not forget who is the foreman and who is the subordinate worker," echoed the voice of Boo and Salami's tormentor.

Boo thought only of the mouse. At a time like this, and under such circumstances, why was he thinking of something as unimportant as a little field mouse.

"Reese, there is a car stopped on the bridge," Fred nervously yelled to his partner. "On the highway, on the bridge, by those far trees."

An arched bridge spanned a lazy river that overlooked the field where Boo and Salami lay still and silent. With it's motor idling, the car's bright headlights reflected against the silver painted girders of the bridge where it had stopped. Steel I-beams and channels, no doubt cast and fabricated at All Steel in Steeltown. A home town that Boo and Salami had left behind, somehow wanting to forget, wanting to leave in their past-memories. Even memories sometimes are best forgotten.

"Let's get out of here . . ., now!" winced Fred.

Reese opened the slip case and placed his companion of destruction into its resting place then zipped the cover closed. Reese and Fred hurried to depart.

In the distance, the Jeep's gears ground themselves because of a loose clutch plate. Boo rested quietly while he listened to the engine fade into the calm of early evening. Against the soft mud, Boo's fingers began to tap to the rhythm of music that could be heard coming from the truck's tape deck. Distant thoughts began to filter through his mind, thoughts of Salami's mother's broken English, the farmer's daughter, Irene. Passionate memories came back. Ziggy, his leg missing and a mind that was wasted, the short life of Frog.

Those Buddy Holly glasses that Frog wore; he was a nerd, somehow, Boo liked him and at times truly missed his presence. More music filled the air across the field, music that Boo had recorded when he and a band played at the Old Empire Hotel. There in the west end of town, the rough and down trodden end of town where life seemed real.

Straining to hear the words, Boo attempted to raise an ear. Those words . . ., those words . . ., he had penned words of his own life, he had lived them, they now had become true to life.

> We raised us some hell.
> Stories and tales, we tell.
> Sowing life's wild oats.
> Over trophies we gloat.
>
> Never regret the lives led.
> Life's burdens cast and shed.
> We raised us some hell.
> Stories and tales, we tell.
>
> I see us not feeble and old.
> In youth, stubborn and bold.

CHAPTER 2
DEAD TOWN

It is not a small town, then again it is not big enough to brag about. A steel mill town, where everything depends on one steel mill to support a town's livelihood. For some men, raised in this steel mill town, depend on a secure job to support their families. It is a hell of a life. For Boo, he gets by, still anticipating something of importance to happen in the future.

Five-thirty on a Monday morning, last night's dreams still linger. It is like a paradise within reach. Outside of a dream, the alarm clock's ringing gets louder and louder until reality is alerted. With a vengeful slap, the clock is nocked into submission.

Yet another week, with the start of another bull-shit session of trying to convince one's self that this is the life. Outside, through the attic apartment window, Boo peers at the sky, filled with a haze of steel plant smog. A cool breeze by midday will have blown the shit farther west of the city. It might turn out to be a nice day, by that time, Boo would be hard at work with no opportunity to glance outside. A steel mill with walls keeps the outside world out, and workers from seeing the daily world passing by.

Boo goes through the same routine every morning, nothing seems to change. Jumping out of bed at five-thirty before the light of day is for the birds. Philosophers and birds think that no one should break a yawn before the rays of light peek over the horizon. Between moans, tosses and turns, Boo curses the whole system. Socks are nowhere to be found; his work clothes are still dirty. Stiff with sweat, they were left standing in the corner of the room since last Friday. Boo had often thought of making-an-effort of bettering himself, or better yet, getting a live-in mate, a woman, someone to be there. As quick as that thought had entered his mind it had faded.

Boo looked around the simple attic apartment; a bed under the sloping roof, a boxed dresser on one wall and a bare light bulb hanging from the ceiling. Behind a drawn curtain was hiding the toilet and bathtub. Wallpaper behind the sink and cupboard no-longer showed its once colorful flowered print. For a moment, Boo's brown eyes tried to focus on the yellowed-white of the small fridge and stove.

'What woman would take to heart a man and a humble abode such as this,' thought Boo to himself. He was beginning to be philosophic. His thoughts rendered them-selves forgotten.

Shit, shower, shave, or shower, shit, shave. Boo could never decide how the saying was suppose to go. When the body is in a stupor, it is funny what unimportant information the mind conjures up and tries to debate rationally. As if that was all, Boo had to contemplate. Shower and shave; he would shit on company time, that was a better and logical decision.

Boo lifted an aching body from the side of the bed, the back slowly began to straighten as a hand reached for the handle of the fridge. A good breakfast surely would be a excellent start to the day, providing that the fridge held a supply of basic food needs. Today, for Boo, the first meal of the day consisted of one raw egg, cracked open into a glass of tomato juice and topped off with a warm beer, the beer as a chaser.

With effort, Boo lumbered into stiff sweat-laden cloths. A glance into a tarnished mirror reflected a young man in his early twenties, tall and lanky with dark brown hair that he combed with work hardened fingers. Tired brown eyes looked back from the mirror, eyes that seemed empty, eyes that needed a change, eyes searching for something that was never in Boo's memory.

Satisfied with breakfast and daily attire, Boo slipped an abused leather coat under an arm and left the attic home. Each step down the side of the house creaked with it's own sound. At night with eyes closed, Boo could tell exactly which step he was on by each step's own unique creak. Those sounds were of welcome, they were the only sounds that greeted him home.

Early morning sounds of vehicles grinding gears, with unburnt gas fumes filling the air around the parking lot leaded to the mill's main gate. Boo pulled the maroon ford half-ton into line behind other early morning workers. Waiting there, watching mindless life inch along, Boo thought of his own worth, what little there seemed to be. 'Everyone stuck in a rut is an ass-hole,' Boo was beginning to include himself in this category.

"No one in this damn place know how to park, park the right way, move your ass jerk!"

"Honk all you want, I'm taking this parking space," yelled Boo from the open truck window.

"You want to make something of it," retorted an upset jerk of a human being from behind the rumbling of an old beat up GM.

After receiving Boo's up turned finger, the GM and driver turned away from the parking space in question. This space was a good one, for this space, Boo would put up a fight. For a brand new truck just off the car lot and a first vehicle for Boo, there was little chance that he would park elsewhere. This space was the best in the lot, the safest. Often the jealousy of others would result in an act of destruction in the form of a key scratch down the length of a vehicle. On some whim, in the mind of a punk, a new truck or sports car would vanish under the cloak of darkness. Boo eased the truck into the parking space.

"Hey Boo, wait up," called a voice from behind a row of parked cars.

Turning around, Boo noticed a well-built guy about five-nine – five-ten in height. A qualified lover by his own informational statements.

"Salami, what the hell you hollering for, it is too damn early in the morning." murmured Boo in a low rumbled voice.

"Where were you the other night? You should have seen the snatch I had."

"You always end up with a dog! A few drinks and your eyes think every dog is a vision of beauty. I take that back, you do not know what beauty is." With a steady pace, Boo headed towards the mill entrance and the punch clocks. Salami tagged along as if he were a homeless ex- pound dog. "An idiot, you are an idiot. Rita was the woman for you, a good loving woman, no other woman I know of is able to give you a home, meals, children." Boo stopped suddenly, turning to face Salami. "Why the hell did you walk out on her?"

"It was not for me, I don't know, I am too young to settle down. I need to be free like you." Salami gestured hands as if his words were a revelation to the free life he thought Boo lead. "Anyway, I've signed the papers. Rita wants to get divorced."

"Ass-hole," was Boo's words spoken into thin air as he continued to walk. "Ass, ass, he doesn't know what life is, what life should be, family." Boo turned his head back to Salami. "Family, you come from a big Italian family, you should know what family means."

"I am not ready, maybe it was a mistake in the first place, Rita cornered me."

In a blink of an eye, Boo's back hand clipped Salami's forehead. A dazed look filled Salami's face, for a moment all thoughts had vanished from his mind.

"You have a kid. Are you willing to just give him up, let him forget that he has a father?" Something in what Boo had said conjured up past memories in his own life. A mother, father, a family for him never existed. In the deepest depths of dreams there is a blank area where memories of a family should be. All that is recalled is an overexposed picture showing shadows for parents. Even the fact that he does not know his real first name, is a game of playful agony. When pressured, or forced to give a name on documents, Boo fabricated extravagant names, then laughed to himself, believing he had fooled people. "You are throwing away your own flesh and blood."

"It ain't going to be like that, I am going to be there for him." Salami stumbled on loose running shoe laces. "Maybe Rita will change her mind, maybe we will get back together, maybe, but just not right now."

From deep in the tangle of steel structures a high pitch whistle of steam cracked the cool morning air. Shift change had begun. Men entering the steel mill from their night of rest met the slaves of the grave yard shift. Tired faces met tired faces of sleep deprived bodies. Below the clanking of steel, the rumble and revving motors, the feet of men shuffled liken to the marching of war weary soldiers.

"Tail is tail, and what the hell is wrong with you? I have never seen you turn down offered tail," Salami boldly forced his opinion into the conversation. Was it a way of trying to force Boo to change the subject about Rita, or force him into another train of thought.

"Do you ever feel that we are going nowhere fast, stuck in a rut. There has to be something better than this. Salami, are you listening to me, do you hear through that thick skull of yours, do you hear what the hell I am saying?"

"Get a load of that ass, Boo!" Salami's blue eyes were glued to a female employee of All Steel. It was evident that several men kept a close eye to the slight sway of hips. To everyone there, those hips were swaying sexually for a purpose. "Nice tight ass."

"Another dog!" exclaimed Boo, while the guy ahead of pounded the shit out of the time card machine.

"Give it a nice gentle kiss, and a rub like this." Boo kissed the tips of his fingers then gently rubbed the time clock's face. Smooth as silk the time clock pooped up Boo's punch card. Exiting boldly past the old guy, Boo entered the graphite filled air. "You have not listened to a word I have said, Salami. It sure is fitting to know that your nick name and mind is a reflection of that dried up meat you tend to eat. What is your lunch today?"

"My dad's home made salami."

"Makes sense."

"Boo, I've heard what you have said."

"Really, enlighten me."

"You said she was a dog."

An aluminum can in front of Boo became airborne from a swift kick. It was unlikely that anyone would pick the can up and dispose of it. For its eternity, it would be kicked from place to place until disintegration rendered it part of the earth of this steel mill. Boo felt that the world had kicked him around over the years.

"You are pissing me off, this job, this mill and this town is starting to piss me off. I am wasting my life working as a laborer in this pit," announced Boo.

Salami's curly blonde hair bounced loosely on his head, hair the girls liked, odd. "So, Boo, what else is there? Don't you need the money like the rest of us?"

"I guess, but that can not be all there is to it, working for the almighty dollar. There has to be life, some-kind of meaningful life, something of importance."

"For me, just money. See you after work, Boo." At a half run, Salami headed towards his work section in the mill.

Green steel clad buildings lined the criss-crossing roads of the steel plant of All Steel. Where else in north America would the largest steel mill cover ten square miles of land. Great lake freighters unload their cargo holes of iron ore pellets, coal and lime at the river docks. West of the main mill, mounds of slag is hauled and piled as a waste product of the steel making process. Visitors from another space world, if landing on the slag heaps, would think of our world as a barren waste land unfit for civilization. If only they knew that our existence is based on great waste for a betterment of mankind, who in return use and abuse created products, then discard the products as waste. In the city of Steeltown, lies such a city that creates the raw steel that mankind turns into consumer products. From open pits, smoke stacks and windowless buildings come billows of heat, smoke and flame, all giving the air and sky a glow of greenish yellow. There is a stench of burnt sulfide. Workers, young and old cough up an industrial cough as they head home to their loved ones, ones they toil for.

Whistles, horns and sirens fought for the same air space. At first, new workers would abide by the warnings, later, the sounds were just a nuisance, shut out of ear and mind. Boo walked the gravel road without listening or paying attention to endangering surroundings. Rumbling past, shaking the earth like an earth quake, a one-hundred-ton slag mover inched close to Boo, sending a dust cloud to surround him.

"Yeah, Salami," said Boo to absent ears. "All he has on his mind is tail, hell who doesn't."

Boo's job of working in the rail mill had to be the most boring job in the steel plant. It was the same procedure over and over, a rail comes down the roller bed a hundred feet long, when the rail reaches the worker, he grabs it with tongs, turns it and sends it on it's way. Nothing new, no new changes, a stagnant labour position.

Like the old Charlie Chaplin movie, 'Modern Times', Chaplin is on the same job day in and day out, hour after hour while the conveyor belt rushes a gizmo past him faster and faster. By the end of the day when work is over, poor Charlie is still walking around moving arms in a mechanical action. Walking home, he is ready to tighten every bolt in sight, or anything that looks like a loose bolt. A comic reaction with a blank dead-pan face.

"Shit, another rail, lets get to work, Charlie," responded Boo to the silent film comic. Turn a rail, push a rail, over and over for hours on end. Looking down the roller bed, there seems to be no end in sight, for the number of rails, one after another keep coming. "Well, Charlie, it is now time to shit on company time." Boo turned to an work buddy and yelled above the clanking of steel against steel, "Hey Peter, watch the rails for me, I am going for a shit."

A grim face smiled with reaction. "Shitting again on company time?"

"Let me know if the foreman wanders by."

"Yeah man, go shit," yelled Pete at the top of his lungs as other workers turned, some smiled and tapped their watches.

It was as if the workers felt that Boo was on a schedule, each day, each shift, on time, shit on company time.

No washroom in this steel plant is a luxurious place to be in, but it is the only place that would give a person a bit of peace and quiet. A place to sit back and visually study the history of the Playboy magazine and centerfold pin ups lining the walls, stalls and ceilings of the john.

"Boo! are you in here?" called out the shift foreman, in less than a polite voice. Boo did not return a reply, his eyes still browsing the Playboy pin-ups. In an abstract mind, Boo was in playboy heaven.

"Get your ass out here! The rails are piling up at your end of the bed." His voice sounding of the devil its self.

"I have my constitutional right, and right now I am taking care of my constitution!"

"Smart ass, get back to work! Before you leave tonight, pickup a letter in my office, it has your name on it."

"What! another twenty-five demerit points?" sarcastically said to the empty room, the foreman had left without waiting for a reply.

Boo slowly and with non existent enthusiasm made his way back to the grind of turning the rail, push the rail, turn the next rail. Charlie and Boo were in an automatic mode of turning rails for the next three hours. What Boo's idle mind was wondering about was the number of demerit points in the hole he had accumulated now. How many points did it take before one was fired or qualified for days off without pay. For Boo, the idea of worrying about money was not of importance. For other men not having money, is a time when they begin to worry. Some men think only of earning money, the more the better.

"Boo!"
"Salami."
"Boo!"

'Why does Salami always repeat my name?' thought Boo, this time he was not going to reply a second then a third time, he would just wait until Salami started to talk.

"Boo! Boo, where are you headed, are you playing ball tonight?" called out Salami from across the plant's parking lot.

Boo waited until Salami was within speaking distance. "No, I ain`t playing ball, I am heading to the Empire Hotel. I, feel a drinking episode coming on."

"What's up? It is kind of early in the afternoon to start a night of drinking." Salami stood by Boo, trying to pull a loose shoe lace from under a foot.

"I am thirsty. You thinking of joining me, or do you have some dog lined up for tonight?"

Salami's comment showed his simple style. "She may be a dog, but she is a purebred."

Boo turned towards the line of parked vehicles, and headed towards his waiting truck as he called back to Salami, "I'll have a couple of cool draft waiting for you."

Standing as if in a state of shambles, the old Empire Hotel occupied the east corner on a street that was once the main business section of a growing town sixty-years earlier. In that time nothing seemed to have changed, it was a drinking hole. Maybe paint had been added to the exterior and modern electricity, other than that the clientele was the same. There was no high-society here, only drinkers, drunks, women of reduced morels and country music of the era. Places like this grow into worlds of their own, dopers, hookers and ass-holes. Did Boo reside here in this simple reality of life? Was he to be swallowed up by this destination of reality?

All bars are the same, with their red beer stained carpets that attract drinkers and entice them to drink more, short skirted barmaids and beat-up arbrite tables. Boo paid no interest in the bar's decor, his eyes were attracted by the shapely legs of a barmaid as she bent down to wipe a table. Salami and a couple of his friends sat close to the band's stage at the east wall. A likely spot for Salami to sit, close to the dance floor, close enough to ogle the women.

A chair was waiting at the table against the wall. In a dive like this, where else was it safe to sit. It was true, that over the past year, Boo was watching his back. After the death of Frog, the air of mystery surrounding the death of Porky in the steel plant, there were accusations of attempted murder pointed towards Boo. All this because of an accident to the shift foreman at number three blast furnace. Reese was shaken, his cloths put aflame, some heat scars that gave his vulgar disposition added character. Boo was cautious, he blamed Reese for the death of Frog, he knew Reese would somehow come after him.

The shapely legged Peg, passed close by Boo, brushing hips against him, "Here Boo, two cool draft just for you." a tempting smile on her lips.

"Thanks Peg." Boo slid a hand over the contour of her well-shaped back end for a moment before she moved happily away. Boo squeezed into the chair. "How have you been Lou, Holly, how was Vegas?"

"He must have had a good time," Lou began laughing. "He hasn't said a word about it since he came back."

"One of them dial-a-hookers," Salami put in. "Must still have Holly's Visa card."

"Come on Holly, tell us about it," Boo began to bug playfully. "Wait until he has had a few drinks, then he will elaborate wantonly."

Holly just sat back, his frail looking body small in the oversized bar chair, a hand slowly mixing the rye set in front. Not a smile on his face, rather a grin that told the others that he had something exciting to revile. After a couple of more drinks, the lustful story would unfold.

Peg's wishful presence at the table was welcomed again when she delivered pickled eggs and drinks. By this time, Holly was eagerly into the Vegas story. With a shyness about him, he waited until Peg had left to serve another table. Among the laughter and seemly remarks, Holly continued his adventure in the land of bliss.

Holly popped up saying, "It is all legal, you just pick up the phone and call one. They even take Master card, I do not have a Visa card, they carry a little credit card machine in their purse."

While Holly continued his pursuit of explanation, and the others taunting him, drinks flowed freely. Pat, one of the members of the band sat down and joined the table, a man of typical Irish heritage with reddish-blonde hair and beard. For over the past year, the group had been a fixture at the Empire. It seemed everyone enjoyed his style of country music. A packed crowd was evidence.

"Another set at nine Pat?" asked Boo.

"About that time, when the other guys show up." Pat accepted the offered beer, Boo had slid in front. "Interested in playing a couple of songs, Boo?"

Through a muffled burp, Boo answered, "After another beer to take the edge off."

"Do you think it will enhance your playing?"

"What is the difference Pat, no one listens anyway, half of the time they are louder than the music."

"All part of the atmosphere. I will call you up to play in the next set. Thanks for the beer." Pat left, tipping the beer bottle to his feathered cowboy hat.

Drinks kept coming to the table, Peg's ass began to look nicer and nicer. Everyone's independent conversation began making less and less sense, Boo downed another beer. With the loud music of the band, a brawl two tables over sounded louder. Some drunk had made a hand pass to a well-stacked girl. Obviously, she resented his looks, her arm sent a beer bottle sailing through the air towards his smug looking face. No-one paid much mind, it was just another fight, time to grab hold of their drinks and make room. After several slaps from both parties, the order of drinking continued.

Through the commotion, Pat's voice echoed from pulsating speaker. "Hey Boo, come on up and do a number, come on." Pat motioned with his pick hand.

There was no incentive from the patrons. Boo had figured he had enough drinking nerves to belt out a song or two. With a push from Salami, Boo managed to squeeze from the table and head to the stage. Staggered applause was not overwhelming, someone was clapping, was it for Boo, or for the outcome of the fight. A burp, a test of the mike, a strum of the guitar, and Boo was ready to perform to a senseless audience. On Boo's guitar strum, Pat and the band picked up the tempo. Slight, then with determination, Boo let his words flow.

> You can't make a living working.
> No you can't make a living working.
> Why waste your time to sit and cry.
> Your days are numbered until you die.
>
> Sing your songs your own way.
> Sing no-matter what they say.
> You can work your fingers to the bone.
> Lord don't waste your days wanting to moan.
>
> Steel town, steel town, here I pay my dues.
> Steel town, steel town, broken life blues.

There was no standing ovation, no deafening applause when the song ended. Hundreds of voices of static gibberish filled the bar beneath the low dark ceiling. Boo wondered if anyone listened to the words, did someone understand the words? With a nod of his head, Boo acknowledged scattered hand claps. Someone was polite enough to reciprocate Boo's efforts.

Taking a deep breath, Boo turned to Pat. "Nature calls, thanks for letting me do my thing. The band did a great back up."

"We will call you up to do another one later, okay." Pat lead the band quickly into a fast country rock song.

Boo's eyes inspected the women and their movements on the dance floor. A perfect opportunity to pick up a bed warmer for the night. Easing into the beer stained chair, Boo slouched limply. 'Another beer,' thought Boo. 'I can handle another beer.'

Holly was still reminiscing about his escapades with a hooker in Vegas. Lou was of no inspiration to Holly's cause, as he teased him about the hooker. Turning with beer foam dripping down the sides of his lips, Salami leaned closer to Boo, at the same time motioned with a limp arm for Peg to bring yet another round.

"What is up with you? It is not too often that you spend the better part of the day in a bar."

"I have a cause to get sloshed." Eyes unable to focus eyed Peg's bottom as she invitingly leaned across the table. "I have one more week of work, then I am out, gone, finished."

"You can't quit!" Concerned, Salami said, wiping foam from lips with a back hand.

Returning an answer with a touch of anger in his voice, Boo blurted out, "I ain't quitting, I was laid off."

"What do you mean laid off! What for? They . . .,"

Boo cut off Salami's train of words, then began revealing the steel mill's reasons why he was being laid off, or as Boo thought, 'Politely fired'. "Too many demerit points. That son-of-a-bitch of a foreman has it out for me. He say's I am using up too much company time shit-ting on company time. The sawed-off bastard!"

"Shit Boo, what are you going to do about it? Fight the demerit points or work the week out? Are you going to put up with that jerk, then just give up?"

"Yeah, I will work the week, but not before I screw him and screw him good." Boo turned a tightened fist, a screw- driver driving a screw home.

Salami's eyes wondered what Boo had scheming in his mind. Back in high-school, anything that went wrong or happened, it was inevitable the blame would be assigned to Salami and Boo. "What are you planning, something good and nasty, I hope."

"I don't know yet, but I will come up with something worthy of my efforts, maybe something memorable."

Soon the others at the table were becoming silent, all wondering what Boo and Salami where talking about. Surely as common working men, they would side with Boo, and encourage him in ways to sabotage the establishment.

"Put sugar in the fuel injection of his Lincoln." Suggested Lou.

"Burn his damn office down, that is what should be done," Holly said, believing more in what he said then in what he would do.

Boo had no specific idea in mind. At this moment, and with alcohol sloshing between ears was no time to make decisions.

Salami needed a towel to wipe the mounting beer foam soaking his chin, again a back hand soaked up the suds. "Like, what are you going to do after you are finished working. I thought you had once said you would probably work your whole life is this shit-hole of a place."

"Hell if I know. Take off and visit a little bit of this big country, hell, I just might get lost in the wilds of Canada. There is nothing in this town keeping me here. No-one holding my heart, no-one keeping me here."

Hours in a day are long when a man spends it drinking in a bar, since shift change, from three o'clock in the afternoon until the last call for rounds. Peg came by calling out last round. Through blurred vision, Boo made out the time to be one-ten, late enough for him. Drinks were downed mouthful by mouthful before each made their way out of the twisted and aged doors.

Night air was crisp and clear, only the distant sounds of the steel mill could be heard over the soft eerie sounds of the crickets. Boo made his way along the parking lot, tall grass felt wet to the touch. Though the fresh air tried to clear Boo's head, the night's alcohol was in command for the duration. To the dampness of the grass, Boo contributed his share of bladder alcohol. Leaning on the tail gate of his capped truck, Boo reasonably decided that driving home to his empty attic apartment was effortless. A simple decision was to crawl into the back of the truck and let instant sleep block out the troubles of the day. All the pains of the day, the realities of the world were left in limbo until the warmth of the sun gently woke Boo from his sleep. Dawn's sun would revive life again with all of it's problems and pains.

Waking in the morning light was not an inspiration to one's head, especially when the body needs to rise but the head stays on the bed. Boo's ravaged body rolled and painfully crawled from the back of his truck. Stiff bones and joints ached as he straightened. Once,

Boo managed to stand erect, his first reaction was to double over and look for a place to fertilize the ground with last night's enjoyment. One can not buy beer, it is only rented out for awhile. Once the rotten sensation was relieved from the pit of his stomach, Boo's morning was still not welcomed. Tucking in shirt-tails and removing the after taste, Boo mustered all faculties. There was one more week of work and some unfinished business to tend to.

Boo turned the truck's key and shuttered when the sound of the motor vibrated into an aching head. Driving the short distance on the curving road, Boo entered the steel mill's parking lot.

As Boo passed the foreman's office, the foreman wasted no time willing to take advantage of flinging an insult. "Boo, you are here nice and early, are you trying to make up for all those lost demerit points." the foreman carried on with a sarcastic voice. "It ain't going to work. You can kiss my ass all you want. You are still going out on your sorry ass."

Boo gave him the finger, then walked on without facing the foreman. "You had better watch your own ass, you are not through with me yet."

"Are you going to work this last week." yelled the foreman through the open office door. "I will give you every dirty greasy hole job in this mill."

Anger flushed on Boo's face as he violently turned to the open door. Was it fear that made the foreman slam the door closed to Boo's barrage of insults? A Steel toed boot made contact to the bottom of the office door as Boo cursed the foreman through the solid steel door. Peeked anger on Boo's face was evidence to other workers when he entered the lunchroom. Tensions were ripe to explode between Boo and the Foreman.

There was no way Boo was going to be intimidated, he would address work the way he had always done it. What else was he to do? There was only one week left.

For the most part, the morning work had gone by without an incident between the two adversaries. Boo felt the need to take his constitutional company shit before he had a real run in with the bastard foreman.

Without warning or provocation, the stall door came flying open from the force of someone's heavy foot. An instant thrust from the door pinned Boo against the back of the john. With pants pulled to hips, Boo lashed out with a foot against the back of the door.

Adrenaline pumping through Boo's veins provided power to send the battered door and assailant sprawling to the floor. Violently, the splintered wooden door was removed by the foreman, there was terror and surprise on his face. The impulse to kick him when he was down was Boo's reaction, he hesitated, pulling back.

"I will wait until I have witnesses in view before I give you an example of pain," said Boo through clenched teeth. There was something of mystery and fear associated with Boo, something that goes boo in the night when one lest expects fright.

"Don't let that stop you."

Boo gathered composure and relaxed the tension affecting every muscle in his body. In a calming voice, Boo said, "There is no hurry, your time will come."

There was a relived relaxation in the foreman's voice. "Then get back to your job."

It was too suspicious of the foreman to just casually say get back to work. He had something else in his mind for Boo. On his way back to the rail bed, Boo pondered the situation as he pulled the loose belt around his waist tight. Boo realized his anger with the involuntary tightness of the belt. Revenge was burning in the depths of his mind, building and flaring for some time. Everything that happened over the past year seemed to be building, as a knot in a stretched wet rope. Thinking about it for days now, Boo concluded that it all started at his high-school graduation, the night Porky flipped the truck and killed Pudden, his own best friend. Though Boo was not friends with Porky or Pudden, somehow he was sorrowful of Pudden's death, a wasted death.

For the time being, there was a calm about the mill. Rails were no longer coming down the bed, no break-down horn sounded. This was a calm, Boo took advantage of. Leaning back on an old stool, Boo pulled the hard hat low over tired eyes. Mill sounds were blotted out by the accustom factor of being exposed to the sounds day after day. Forty winks of sleep would be of welcome, compared to the sleepless night received. Unknown to Boo, during the siesta, the rails were now moving down the roller bed. Suddenly, the stool vanished from beneath, hands grabbed at his shirt front attempting to haul him to his feet. A fist was the instant reaction that connected to the face of the grabber.

"You son-of a bitch, your time has come," came the voice from under the green hat of management.

Boo reached behind and grabbed hold of the stool's leg, the swinging follow through bringing a cracking sound on impact. Hitting the cement floor was the clinking sound of a fiberglass hard hat.

"Hold on Boo!" Salami came running up from the other side of the bed.

Boo had landed one fist to the jaw of the foreman, his body limply sprawling across the landing.

Salami had reached Boo, and attempted to restrain Boo's efforts of striking another blow. "He is down, get out of here! In short time, there will be green hats all over the place all ready and willing to screw you bad." Pulling a resisting Boo, Salami headed down the hallway towards the nearest exit. Salami's face was in a sweat, as was an irate Boo. "Clear out before someone calls security." Salami looked back with a concerned frown. "What the hell did you have in mind?"

"I had no time to think. I had it up to here with him." Catching a breath, Boo wiped at sweat above a brow. "Look Salami, I have had enough of this mill, and this one mill town. I am getting out."

"Out where?"

"Out of this town. West, I'll head west."

The look on Salami's face showed a train of entertaining thoughts.

"If you are interested, I will drive by your place after I take care of a few things." Taking a breath, Boo added. "Be ready, if you are interested in a new adventure."

Boo pushed through the doors towards the outside world, he did not turn his head back towards Salami or the mill. "As far as I am concerned, this is a dead town."

Steel against steel sounded for the last time in Boo's ears, the last sound among the various sounds of the steel making process, the last sound of steel doors of the steel mill closing behind him. Freedom.

CHAPTER 3
SHIT HAPPENS

There was no reason or even logic behind the incident in the rail mill between the foreman and Boo. Boo did not have a reason to run, or a reason to fear anything or anyone. He was running from something. Whatever it was, his mind was made up, he was on his way following the highway lines to whatever destination.

Boo wasted little time removing himself from the premises of All Steel, he hurried some-what cautious of what the situation might be like in the mill. Instincts favored a fast exit. Black rubber from heated tires left tread marks on the paved parking lot. Boo looked straight ahead, paying no attention to stop signs, traffic lights or incidentals in his path. Thoughts were on escape, leaving a vast space between himself and the perils of the steel mill.

In the small attic apartment, only essentials were being gathered. Uncleaned clothes were stuffed into a brown paper bag, music tapes, a razor, the necessities. From a tin can, Boo had grabbed cash savings and placed it into a compartment of a guitar case below the black guitar. Nothing else of importance was worth taking, for that matter, nothing of importance was left behind. With life belongings in arms, Boo stepped down the staircase, listening to the unique sound each step made. As if placing the sounds into a memory, Boo counted off the steps in descending order. Stopping at the bottom of the steps, Boo scratched a message on a note and placed it between the glass panes of the door. A simple note to the landlord stating, 'gone on vacation, Boo'. Short and sweet, and to the point. As far as Boo was concerned there was nothing else to say and no questions were needed to be asked.

With caution, Boo drove up to Salami's mother's house. Pausing at the end of the driveway, with a foot lightly on the brake, Boo looked towards the open door of the house. There seemed to be no-one home. Suddenly, Salami exited with a bundle of clothes in arms, behind him, came his mother stomping, yelling and carrying on about something. With a dish towel in hands, she began to flog Salami in a comical manner.

"Leave your Mama, leave your baby, and Rita, leave, you no son of mine no more!"

Salami hobbled along the sidewalk beside the moving truck, dropping pieces of clothes along the way. Boo laughed at a comical, rather hurtful and sad situation. Salami was following Boo's escape, but was it a necessary escape for Salami. A loving mother flogged her son after picking up his dropped clothes and stuffing them back into his arms.

Salami's mother slapped him on the back, between sobs into the dish towel and calling out, "Who's gonna take care of you. You have clean underwear, case you get into an accident? I beat you, you come back home all hurt from an accident."

"Yes Mama, I will be careful," replied Salami while stuffing belongings into the back of the truck while trying to elude his mother's loving strikes from the dish cloth.

Mother pushed Salami into the open truck door then slammed the door in his face. Boo tried to hold back a building laughter, it was becoming impossible. The urge to laugh ceased when thee woman ran to driver's side of the truck and began poking a finger at Boo. Boo tried hard, not to stare directly into the woman's eyes.

"You, Mr. Boo, be careful eh. Don't let Francis get into no bad trouble. You listen to Mrs. Frankano."

"Yes, Mrs. Frankano, we will be careful," That was all Boo was able to say without cracking up into laughter, he could not think of anything else.

"You two have a good time. You are still young and foolish. Now go, before I start to cry."

Boo eased the truck away from the sidewalk. From the side mirror, he could see Mrs. Frankano, with a dish-towel to her nose, sniffling as she cleaned the sidewalk with shuffling feet.

Like fools, Salami and Boo sat stiffly while driving through town, not saying a word. Both had something to think about, and needed a moment to collect their thoughts. Once on the open highway their mood would change. Left behind would be headaches, heartaches and forgettable memories of life working in a steel mill. On the open highway they would follow a direction with no destination in mind. Westward, away from All Steel, Steeltown and a past life. Go west young man. A corny saying, but for Salami and Boo, going west meant excitement and adventure that all young men craved.

"Francis, ha . . ., ha . . ., where did you get a name like that?" Boo could not resist any longer, the laughter just came. Salami just presented a blank expression. "A name like Francis, ha . . .!"

"Funny, very funny," Salami laughed the humor off. It was obvious that he hated the name.

Throughout the years they knew each other, neither one knew the other's real first name. Boo agreed that the name Francis did not suit Salami, Salami was Salami.

"So, you think it is funny, eh Boo?"

"Yeah, kind of."

"So, then tell me your real name?"

"You know my name Salami. It is Joe, just plain old Joe, nothing else, just Joe."

"Bull-shit!" Salami was not at all satisfied.

Both were beginning to relax; the tensions of the day were fading. Only one last situation remained in Boo's mind. What had happened after leaving the plant? What would happen if and when Boo returned to town? Salami was there and had some idea of what transpired afterwards.

"Hey Boo, about today, and the things that went on. I don't know all the reasons, but I am behind you all the way man."

"Thanks."

"You really bopped that foreman. I can tell you that he is out to get you. He said he would have cut your water off if he could have gotten his hands on you."

"A real pervert."

"He would have needed a couple of goons to do his dirty work," said Salami with a slight imitation of feminism in his voice. "He is the only one to worry about, security was not informed."

"I ain't worried, see . . ., I ain't shaking." Boo raised a hand and slightly shook it for effect.

On the curving and hilly highway of Trans-Canada highway seventeen, Boo and Salami settled into a relaxing speed. The once anxiousness began to become an ease of mind and body. About twenty-miles from town, the boys stopped at a gas station and beer store just across the bridge crossing the Goulais river. All the boys needed was gas and beer, the next watering hole would be in the small town of Wawa, a three hour drive north west of Steeltown. The late afternoon highway traffic was beginning to decrease as the supper hour rolled around.

Highway seventeen's black top, with it's endless yellow lines gave off the heat waves of the day. Slowly sinking, behind the tree tops covering the landscape, the sun's gleam faded into the evening hours. Passing by the truck's window, the scenery was the pride and envy of a photographer's camera lens. Soon the rocky hills and variety of trees would be cast into the blackness of night. In the night, only the eyes of creatures roam, man seeks the security of shelter.

Salami leaned back, grabbing some shut-eye as the last of the sun's rays disappeared. An empty beer can slipped through the relaxing hand. Boo listened to the words being sung on the tape playing in the tape deck. A song Boo and Pat had recorded at the Empire Hotel. In the silence of the truck, Boo seemed to be hearing the words for the first time, it's meaning began to take on a new life. Boo turned up the volume and leaned back with a comfort he had not had in some time. As if live at the Empire Hotel, Boo began to mouth the words to the recording.

> Lazy old dreams, never come true,
> But when I am dreaming, I'm never blue,
> How about you?
>
> I'd like to be a cowboy,
> Ride across the plains,
> Or be a lonesome Hobo,
> Riding long freight trains.
>
> Or be a lanky farm boy,
> Dreaming summer dreams,
> Farming the green valley,
> Beneath prairie moon beams.
>
> I'd like to be a rambler,
> Traveling across this land,
> And searching for a lady,
> Yearning for this man.
>
> I'd like to spend our time,
> On an old porch swing,
> In the darkness of the night,
> Not doing a darn thing.

Lazy old dreams, never come true,
But when I am dreaming, I'm never blue,
How about you?

    The night continued with a sense of emptiness. Boo watched the darkness of the night passing by the truck's window as if it were a dream of empty visions. With Salami sleeping against the passenger door, Boo also was beginning to feel the wanting of sleep. About a mile from the town of Wawa, Boo pulled the truck into the empty parking lot of an abandoned gas station. After crawling into the back of the truck and opening a beer, Boo sat in silence, listening to the echoes of the night. Far from his mind and ears were the sounds of the city and the clanking of steel against steel at the mills of All Steel. Steeltown no-longer existed, the town and mill were no-longer of importance. Boo pried the top off of another cool Canadian, the tartness of alcohol and beer yeast itched at his dry throat.

    'Wawa', sounds like something a child would say when they want water. It sounds like a funny name to give a town, maybe it is a funny town. At a curve in the highway of seventeen and the road turning towards Wawa stands a huge statue of a Canadian goose. Standing over twenty feet from wedded feet to head, give or take a few feathers, this statue stands guard at the entrance to the little northern Ontario town. Named after the goose, the town took its name from the native Canadian word for geese.

    Standing tall on a hill above the lower highway, the goose stands in a ready to fly pose. If people driving along the highway were not paying attention one would be apt to feel the wind beneath the big bird's wings. Why not? People see flying saucers everyday. Passing beneath the tail feathers, the road leading into town winds it's way into the northern Ontario mining town. An iron ore town that mines a basic ingredient that All Steel uses in the steel making process.

    Morning came with welcome, the sun's rays of warmth filtered through the back window of the maroon truck sitting lonely in the parking lot. For Boo, waking up after the sun had been up for an hour was a change in life. After working shiftwork, one's internal clock is affected. Fighting back blinking eyes, Boo crawled from the tail gate of the truck to welcome the day and its life healing rays. Fresh air entered lungs, air that seemed different. Standing there for the first time, Boo felt alive, with a sense of beginning to feel new. All the memories, of the past life of growing up living and working in Steeltown, and of lost friends seemed to be discarded, as if unwanted clothes.

Boo walked to the passenger door. "Salami, wake up, breathe the fresh air of freedom. No work, no ass-hole foreman," said Boo pulling the door open on a dazed Salami.

Tumbling out onto weak legs, Salami staggered to his feet. With a sour faced grin, Salami fought the stale taste of beer in his mouth. Eyes studied the two empty beer bottles in his hands. "A toast to the good times, and the hell we are going to raise." Salami turned the empty bottles over. "I think we need refills."

"Shit who needs it. This is a new beginning, I do not need or want an artificial high to enjoy; look fresh air, clear skies, it will not give you a hang-over or cotton-mouth." Boo was beginning to sound like a converted atheist.

"What? Boo is that you . . ., are you in there, Boo?" questioned Salami, following Boo who wandered about as if possessed. "Are you giving up drinking?"

"This is my drinking, I am going to drink the nectar of life." Boo began to empty the truck of loose beer bottles and the case of beer in the back of the truck. "We just piss it away anyway."

With two empty beer bottles in his hands, Salami followed as if a desperate man seeking the last drop of beer on earth. It was not happening, Boo could not be in his right mind, yet he tossed out every last bottle from the truck. In a daze, Salami walked around, stepping over the bottles as if they were sacred objects of worship. With open arms and hands clenched tightly on the bottles of beer, Salami silently questioned Boo.

Being satisfied that the truck was completely empty of beer bottles, Boo ceremoniously unzipped his pant's fly and began to anoint the discarded beer bottles. "I piss on you with my last rented beer."

From the highway, passer-byes observed the ritual, but in no way understood the birth of a new feeling within Boo's mind and soul. Salami was as bewildered as the gawking tourists, then again Salami is easily bewildered.

Boo shook the last drop of converted beer from his penis. "There, that is the last beer I am going to rent." With a sense of relief and satisfaction, Boo zipped up then climbed into the drivers seat.

Breaking the morning quietness, the engine roared to life, the wheels of the truck grabbed then kicked the loose gravel on the lot. "Salami . . ., you interested in coming along for the ride."

A betrayed look was on Salami's face, he hesitated a moment before feet began to race towards the moving truck. Making a decision on the fly was not easy for Salami. Missing a ride was more important than the beer he was leaving behind. Quickly Salami released the bottles in his hands, and clutched the open door of the moving truck. Hauling himself in, Salami took a last look towards the beer bottles left behind. "Hey Boo, I . . ., I did not get a chance to piss away my rented beer." Salami squirmed with a full bladder.

Passing under the tail feathers of the Wawa goose, the boys made their way into the small town of Wawa. Being tourists was not yet in the boy's thoughts. More important was the need to find a restaurant with facilities. Having the company-john, and time, was no-longer at their disposal.

"Pick a restaurant, Salami."

"One two buckle my shoe, that one is good enough for me," said Salami in a hurried voice.

Salami did not welcome the quick turn of the truck into the restaurant parking lot, or the sudden stop. An ocean of waves surged back and forth in his bladder. Before Boo could turn the ignition off, Salami rushed out and into the restaurant, no doubt he hastened to the facilities. Boo combed shoulder length hair with spaced fingers, fussed with the shirt collar before entering the establishment, acting as nonchalant as possible. Being an obvious tourist was not what he intended.

Taking a seat at a booth, Boo eyed the waitress strolling over in a suggestive manner. She smiled as she took out a note pad and began to ask for a order when Salami stumbled into a seat after stepping on loose running shoe laces.

"May I take your order."

"Oh sorry, excuse me," said Salami.

"Well, I will have two eggs sunny side up. And since we just arrived in town, I will have two toast and the location of this town's night spot. Also, I would like, if I may, a tall glass of tomato juice with pepper, malt vinegar, and the yoke, just the yoke of an egg stirred in not shaken. If you are interested, I would like someone to show us a good time tonight Miss . . . ?

"Miss . . ., Sue, Sue Halls," she answered with a hesitant tone.

"What time do you finish, get off work?"

"Six o'clock, but," her mouth dropped open in a stupefied pose, she turned to make an exit when Salami called after her.

"If you have a friend, I will have the same, and the same food order as my friend," called Salami after the retreating waitress.

Sue turned, smiling as she answered, "Yes."

Breakfast came promptly with a bit of added personal care. Boo eyed the tomato concoction then downed the contents in one swallow. This, he hoped, would be the last time he would require an antidote remedy for beer drinking hangovers. Boo and Salami finished their meal and handsomely thanked the waitress with a tip. Boo reminded Sue of their date.

"We will see you at six."

"Yes okay, bye . . ., wait. What is your name?"

"I am Boo, and this is Salami."

"Those are odd names!" she noted, as the boys exited.

Boo turned, smiled and answered simply and honestly, "Yes they are, and we are a little odd at times."

A feeling of a hot spell was in the air. A day where one would attempt to do nothing but sit back in the shade and watch the world go by. Boo was beginning to agree with this philosophy of life. Locating a shady tree to recline beneath, Boo and Salami indulged in the passtime of lounging. At a time before, they would have indulged in the exercise of bending the elbow, lifting a beer bottle from stomach to lips. Though Salami fidgeted, uncertain as to what to do with his hands and mind, he did not request the need to have a beer. This pleasure, of rest and letting the wonders of the world enter senses, Boo welcomed with an open mind and dissolving eyes.

Sue began to create a habit of looking out of the restaurant window, starting at about five o'clock. Deep inside her mind, she told herself that those boys would not show up. Her heart hoped that they would. Why does a heart sometimes over-rule the mind? 'Why?' Sue questioned herself, but she wanted to follow her heart rather than the strictness of her mind. That was what her father wanted her to follow, the mind, always follow the mind.

"Cathy, come here," called Sue to a best friend. "Those guys I was telling you about." Sue continued to gaze out through front window. "They are here, they came back."

"Where are they?" Cathy tried to get a glimpse of Salami and Boo, as she leaned over the counter. In her excitement she knocked over several milk glasses with her abundance of chest.

"Cathy, see that maroon truck with the pin stipes and wooden running boards!"

"Yeah, but I do not see the guy you want to set me up with. That guy you call a hunk of meat. What is his name?"

"His name is Salami, he is just named after a hunk of meat. Don't ask me why!" Sue raised arms in an unknowing manner. "He is not bad looking, for a guy. What do you say, will you come with me?"

"I don't know, I . . ., maybe."

"Great, thanks Cath."

When six o'clock finally arrived, the two girls slowly made their way over to Boo's parked truck. Life's preliminaries of introductions and small talk were carried out before all felt comfortable about each other. Before the night's entertainment at the local night spot, they all squeezed into the truck and headed to the local A & W for hamburgers and the original root beer.

While sipping root beer and devouring hamburgers more small talk was made before the girls began to relax. In the close quarters of the truck's cab it was hard to be relaxed when bodies were so close.

Sue started the interrogation, "Where did you ever get a name like Boo?"

Boo lowered his head then peered up under frowning eye brows, reflecting an emptiness deep in the brown colour.

"See, do you see," egged on Salami's voice. "See the ghost deep in his eyes."

"I do," proclaimed Cathy. "I just felt a shiver up my spine."

Sue saw the haunting hiding behind the soft eyes, she refused to accept anything evil.

"Booooo . . .," said Boo, with a teasing tremble from deep in his throat.

Cathy gave a little squeal, "I felt something." She edged away from Salami.

"I think you should be afraid of Salami," implied Sue.

"I would be a little worried about his mind," suggested Boo, laughing. "And you should not be afraid of his anatomy, his appendage has no relevance to the sausage he has been nicknamed after."

Sue laughed readily, then Cathy caught on and laughed with slight embarrassment. It seemed that the ice had been broken. With the consumption of food, the friendship of people are made at ease, this transition was happening between the four new acquaintances.

Boo watched Sue walk to her house to freshen up for the evening. Sue's blonde hair flowed past shoulders in a light wisp, her legs straight and long. Boo thought different of her, not in the same way he had used Peg at the Empire Hotel.

Salami, on the other hand, thought only of one thing, and commented on Cathy's assets. Cathy was not a bar maid as Salami had hoped for, she had wholesome values and yet beauty that Salami would not notice. Salami had missed the beauty of Rita, and now he had lost Rita.

Like the heat of the day, the night would continue with the same passion. With the same acceptance of the day, Boo intended to make of the night. Entering the local establishment for fun and entertainment, Boo felt the sameness of the Empire Hotel in Steeltown; music, drinking, drunks and potential fights. After being accustomed to this type of life style, Boo did not know how else to entertain.

Boo was determined to let life entertain him. While the others ordered drinks, he favored a non alcoholic drink. With the ease of the locale, Sue gave Boo the impression of being available and willing. On the other hand, Salami was in difficulty with Cathy who averted every advance by pulling away and tugging at her sweater. Salami continued to apply awkward charm which Cathy had no problem controlling. While the evening continued with dancing, laughter and innocent foreplay, Boo sought a different excitement, something of more substance.

"Sue," spoke Boo over the decibels of the rock band. "What is in this town, other than this, for excitement? I am hoping for something different."

"Not much." There was a glow in her eyes. "What would you like to do?"

"Make out?" Boo answered quickly. Sue's answer was just as quick.

"Not yet, Boo," said Sue in a hopeful passionate way.

Salami tried hard to impress Cathy. Coming on with every move and line he could think of, he was striking out big time.

Suddenly out of the blue an idea struck Boo. It would be exciting, something to do. Boo asked Sue in an excitable voice. "What time do the tourists usually go to see the duck . . ., I mean the goose. What time do they start to gather?"

"About eight or nine in the morning I guess, why?"

"I have an idea, Sue. Come on Salami, and Cathy, you too." They all got up reluctantly, each questioning Boo as to what he was doing. "Trust me." He said. "Up and go."

From the static of everyday events in the bar, the four headed into the night of expected escapades that Boo was conjuring up. Boo began to give his companions a list of materials they would need. Beneath the haze of heat held close to the earth, Boo and innocent followers were willing to heat up the night even more.

"We need some paint, red, white and yellow. Paint brushes and shovels. Also," Boo brought his voice to a crescendo. "Also, some good shit, not old shit, but fresh shit, good old cow manure. Are you all ready?"

All heads turned to acknowledge a sense, of a lack of understanding. All were in agreement that they were game.

"Okay, where can we find some paint, paint brushes and shovels?"

Cathy was hesitant. "My father's garage has all that stuff, but I do not know where we are going to find manure."

Fresh cow manure could be found later, after they retrieved the essentials from Cathy's father's garage. There was no lights on in the house when Boo eased the truck to a stop in-front of the driveway of Cathy's house. A moment passed before they moved towards the garage. Silent footsteps in the damp grass gave out a sound that the four thought could be heard for miles. After each step, the thieves paused then inched towards the garage. A mad scramble was made to the garage door, they pressed their backs flat against the garage wall. Sounds of a rusted door knob screeched as Salami turned the handle.

"This is easier than I thought. The door opened just like that. Would anybody happen to have a flashlight on them?" Each gave the same negative answer with a sway of their heads. "How about a lighter?" the same negative answer was given.

Cathy suggested in a normal pitched voice, uncommon to a thief on the job. "Why don't you turn on the light switch, it is on your left."

All looked at Cathy with unemotional faces. She raised shoulders, smiling arrogantly. Salami flicked on the light switch without further adieu. In the brightness the rummaging began for the needed implements. The more they looked, the more the noise increased as other materials were tossed about. Everyone froze in position when a foreign voice was heard outside of the garage.

"Is that you Frank. What is all the noise about?" asked Cathy's father from the font door of the house.

No one moved, no one uttered a syllable. Boo began pointing a finger at Cathy, trying to get her to say something. Cathy did not understand until Sue gave her a poke, bringing her back to reality. The moment lingered.

"It is me Dad, I am . . ., I am putting my bike away."

"Okay, but do you have to make so much noise? I will leave the door open for you."

Boo sighed with relief. "It was about time you said something. It would be kind of hard to explain our presence."

"It is going to be hard enough trying to explain why I was putting my bike away. I do not own a bike!"

Laughter was kept down to a minimum while the gathering of loot for the night's adventure continued. Making off with paint, brushes and shovels, the four gave the impression of low-class thieves making their escape across the front lawn. A delay occurred as Cathy ran back to the house to close the door left open for her entrance.

Now the only thing left to find was fresh cow manure. In the early morning hours the truck and it's passengers searched the back roads looking for a farm or even a barn with a few cows. Night's darkness was now showing the lightness of the coming dawn. Would there be time to carry out Boo's little prank before the tourists began arriving to see the goose. Finally Sue pointed out a barn hidden down a winding road. Encumbered by the shovels, the night stalkers headed towards the barn, their noses affirmed that there were cows present.

"Lots of fresh shit here. Let's go!" Boo said boldly as he opened a side door of the barn.

Weathered old boards creaked on rusty hinges. Soft mooing came from the resting cows. Reluctantly, the rest of the group followed Boo into the barn. Cathy and Sue pinched their noses closed, and tried to breath through tight lipped mouths.

"Okay, begin work. Shovel up as much shit as you can carry." Boo dug a shovel into a gooey pile of manure that was steaming behind a milk cow, locked in a neck yoke.

Sure, that they were willing to see the prank through, Boo felt their eyes looking at his back as if he were nuts; maybe he was. Life does need a little bit of excitement once in awhile.

Salami piped up, "Where do we put all this shit we dig up, in our pockets."

In mid scoop, Boo paused, aware that he had forgotten the mode of containment. After a quick glance through the dimly lit barn, Boo noticed empty feed bags. "Yeah, in those empty feed bags over there. Fill them up with good fresh green shit."

Sue and Cathy held the bags open while they tried turning their heads away to breath in short breaths of pungent air. Boo and Salami wandered behind the stalled cattle shoveling up the wet manure.

Sue began to say through a held breath as she twisted the bag closed, "This shit smells like shit, it is terrible. What are we going to do with it?"

"Trust me!"

"Okay, but I ain't going to touch it."

"Me either!" sounded Cathy as she turned up her nose in disgust.

Salami's voice came to her rescue, "You don't have to, I will carry it for you."

In the short hour, the group had seven feed bags filled with aromatic manure. Four trips were made back and forth until the bags were loaded into the back of Boo's truck. The girls carried the shovels at arms length, then spent time rubbing their shoes in the tall grass. Boo's scheme was now ready to be put in motion. Their destination was the great big goose across town where the majestic bird stood in picturesque glory. On the way into town, Boo unraveled the results of everyone's efforts. All were in agreement that the tourists would be surprised and baffled by the prank's outcome.

Silently, sitting there under the moon's glow, the goose paid no attention to the goings on behind its back. Then again, a noble bird would care. At this time, of early morning, the highway was void of traffic. With the hour of four in the morning there was enough of the moon's light to let the deceivers carry out their prank. Salami and Cathy took the yellow paint and began painting behind the goose to the centre of the highway. Their job was to paint giant goose foot prints on the highway, and on the grass leading up to the goose. With red and white paint in their hands, Boo and Sue headed further up the highway. On the several road signs leading towards the statue of the goose, they painted an advancing message onto the signs. When their tasks were completed they gathered on the highway behind the tail feathers of the goose.

"Now for the main ingredient," Boo mimicked in a mad professor accent. "Bring me the fresh smelly five-dollar a pound shit, but only the good mushy shit."

Salami bent over and hunched his back as the hunch back of Notre Dame. "Yes master, your wish shall be done sire."

"Good, but do not forget the shovel. I hate to use my hands, it leaves a distasteful smell that lingers and lingers and lingers."

In a girlish giddy manner, the girls pranced around as if they were now only eight-year-olds being naughty for the first time. Boo shoveled the manure into piles in a scattered pattern along the highway. In the distance, the early rays of the coming day's sun turned the grey sky into a hazy blue.

"Our job is done. Now we wait until morning when the tourists begin to arrive," proudly said Boo, as he glanced back over their handy work.

After gathering their implements into the truck, Boo parked the truck in the visitors parking lot. Taking a blanket with him, Sue followed him to a grassy patch under a pine tree. Salami and Cathy crawled into the cab of the truck with Salami intent on making time. Salami's hand brushed through Cathy's long auburn air with a passionate intent. Tonight there would be no passion, not in Cathy's mind.

Blue of the sky began to show its colour, as the early morning hours came. A heavy dew made the grass feel cool and wet to the touch. Boo paid no attention to a small detail as he laid the blanket onto the grass and beckoned Sue to lay beside him. Reaching up with an open hand, Boo softly took Sue's uncertain hand and drew her to his side. Warm soft lips touched. Fingers weaved through silky blonde hair. Sue's eyes questioned not what she wanted answers of. She wore no bra, Boo's hands investigated her shapely body, the small of her back, the firmness of her rear that curved gently into thighs held tightly together. Sue pulled the end of the blanket over them. Beneath the blanket body warmth fought off the chill of the night. What was anticipated was not foreseen. Sue pulled him closer until warm skin lay against warm skin. This moment spoke for its self. Today or the next, Boo and Salami would be on their way. This night a delight in ecstasy to recall in memory.

Where they lay, the morning sun warmed their bed. In Sue's eyes, she gave a glowing reflection. Not a word was spoken. The memory of the past hours brought on a new burning desire. A touch of a hand on her cheek, with a tender kiss on warm soft lips, told her that there was not to be a lasting romance. With Boo and Salami's departure the routine of life, for her, would continue on unchanged.

But, last night's antics brought a change to the norm, an excitement the girls longed for. Today the results of their efforts would affect the town and the tourists visiting the Wawa goose. Gathering their composure, Boo and Sue joined Cathy and Salami back at the truck. Deep in sleep in each other's arms they were found to be, a smile was etched on Salami's lips. Had he scored?

Grabbing the mirror and door handle, Boo began to rock the truck. "Good morning sweet things."

Cathy, startled to consciousness, checked to see that her clothes were on and properly fastened. Repeatedly, she pushed Salami's head away from her bosom until he woke. A grin on his face faded, then soon appeared, then disappeared when Cathy sternly gazed at him.

"Up and at it. It is about time to see the effects of our efforts." Boo opened the passenger door to let the love birds fall out.

On the lower highway, the day's traffic was beginning to increase. Tourists would soon be making their way to this attraction as they do to every attraction listed on travel brochures. No-one seems to study and take in the culture of an area, they rush from one exhibit to another taking endless pictures as proof of the good times they had. To some, the great Wawa goose was just another marvel to take a picture of before heading to the next town.

The most expensive of expensive Cadillacs had brought an elderly couple to the northern parts of Ontario. Mrs. Fonsworth, of the Boston Fonsworths', was not in favor of this trip. On all accounts, she wished to be back in Boston where everything was handed to her on a silver platter. This adventure of her husband's, she wanted no part of. A diamond ring covered hand frantically fanned her laden face.

"Mr. Willis Fonsworth, please engage the automobile's air-conditioner to dispense of this terrible stench." pouted Mrs.

Fonsworth, as she placed an expensive silk handkerchief to her nose. A forceful voice demanded, but she did not raise her dignified voice above her social upbringing. "Mr. Fonsworth."

"That is clean fresh air Kate, enjoy it, take a deep breath." Mr. Fonsworth lowered his wife's side window by remote control, he took in a deep breath. "Clean Canadian air."

"Willis Fonsworth . . ., you are highly infuriating!" she said, with a touch of disgust in her voice, then turned her head away.

Willis grinned even wider at his wife's turmoil. This was his adventure. Anyway, after years of giving into his wife's whims, he had given up many a vacation, he now had it his way, and was going to make the best of it.

Turning onto the bypass highway leading into Wawa, Willis noticed the odd coloured signs. Curiosity had the better of him as he slowed just enough to read each sign. Willis read aloud to his discontented wife.

"That sign reads, 'WATCH OUT' the next says, 'FOR FALLING' and the third reads, 'GOOSE DROPPINGS'." At that moment, both Mr. And Mrs. Fonsworth The Third, looked skyward through the windshield. Expecting, no doubt, to see a goose flying over, doing the unexpected.

As if the car had entered the depths of winter's wet slush, came a sound and feeling just as familiar. The most expensive of expensive silver Cadillacs ran over the mounds of manure placed along the highway. Mr. Fonsworth held the vehicle under control while it slipped and slid on manure as glazed as black ice on a highway's black top in the depths of winter.

A dignified Mrs. Fonsworth, was in a squeamish state, she covered her face with a silk handkerchief. "Willis Fonsworth this is the end, you will send me home on the first flight to Boston!"

Frantically, Mrs. Fonsworth began to fan the air, her nose and lips squirmed into an ugly sneer. By now the acrid smell of fresh manure began to filter into the car. Surely the stickiness of the manure would adhere to the tires for hours. At first Willis was concerned with the sliding car, then once it was under control, he began to smile at the outcome of someone's prank.

Grinning more than ever, he saluted the goose as he steered the Cadillac towards town. Turning to his wife, and with a slate blank face he asked, "What is the matter my Dear, is something bothering you?"

"You know perfectly well what is definably wrong. You will let me go back to Boston." Disgust showed in every wrinkle on her face.

Willing to happily and lovingly torture his wife, Willis lowered all the car windows to receive the full extent of the smell. "There are no large planes in this area my Dear." Willis drove on smiling from ear to ear.

Soon other cars came through with the same gusto, families stopped to watch others. Humor is accepted, even when it is a disgusting occurrence, so say the victims of the gathered audience. Children of a family in a station wagon wanted to stomp through the goose droppings. An old farmer in a beat up old truck sailed through without noticing anything out of the ordinary, he spat tobacco out of the side window.

Under the heating morning sun, the smell began to intensify and spread over the entire area. Boo, Salami and the girls watched from a distance, their pleasure was in the laughter shared between themselves, and the mounting crowd. People were having fun, it was a change from the mundane, a change from the boring pictures of statues meaning nothing.

Like all festivities, there is someone that takes offence. Sirens cut through the festive air as the sound of approaching police cars came from the town's direction. The fun was over. Boo started the truck while the others clambered in. Haste was not made, in a slow pace the truck passed the police cars on its way into town. If they held an innocent look on their faces there would be no questions asked. Leaving town was still a good idea for Salami and Boo.

Goodbyes were short, there were no long-term commitments. A kiss, a gaze into each other's eyes, no words spoken. Boo softly touched Sue's loose hair, then slowly dropped hands to his side. There was emotion in Boo's heart, but now, and here was not the time, Boo was still searching to find himself.

Salami gave Cathy unintended promises as he had done times before. Hopefully she was able to see through Salami's false intentions. Boo started the truck then gave a last smile towards Sue. Her face, its lovingness was stored in Boo's subconscious. Behind the restaurant, stood Sue and Cathy with the evidence of the night's antics. Shovels, paint and feed bags smelling of manure surely would convict the innocent girls of a small town.

Taking the back road out of town then onto highway seventeen, Boo and Salami headed west towards the next town. Unlike the troubles, they had in Steeltown, and the fun they had in Wawa, it was obvious that different kinds of shit happens.

CHAPTER 4
POLICE CHIEF'S DAUGHTER

Nothing but heat could be felt, the day was beginning to take its toll on the many tourists traveling the long stretch of Highway Seventeen West. Cars were pulling off the crowded highway, looking for rest stops for relaxation. Weary travelers were taking in the oasis atmosphere of cool shade trees, and the rushing flow of cool river water that would feel tantalizing upon the naked skin. Picnic tables covered with appetizing food and refreshments would satisfy the hunger pains of an empty stomach.

Boo pulled the ford truck into a rest stop along the highway. By chance, would someone offer two weary travelers a bit of substance. Salami and Boo were traveling light, they had not planed well for this trip. Each day came, to be dealt with at that moment. A chance to wash their summer dried faces, in the cold waters of a river flowing from as far north as one can imagine, would be of welcome.

People looked with wonder when the truck pulled into the rest stop, their domain. Tourists that were once filled with laughter had now become quiet. Without making it noticeable, they would glance at Boo and Salami from the corner of their eyes. It was not until Boo and Salami smiled and said hello, did the other people respond with kind. Friendly conversations slowly broke the ice. Road talk among the men was a male bond that eased the apprehensive tensions that strangers have towards each other.

After Boo and Salami had washed up a bit in the cool water of the passing river, they were offered a snack and drinks. Boo gave the tourists a history of the area and the routes of the northern highways. On their departure, strangers bid adieu to friendlier strangers. Salami stretched out in the back of the truck as Boo pulled their transportation onto the northern highway. A welcomed cool breeze flowed through the open windows of the truck as the boys headed to the next little town of Marathon.

Times have changed over the years, also the life styles of the younger people have changed. Back nine or ten years previous, the sides of the highways were clustered with hitchhikers. Everyone it seems, people between the ages of sixteen and twenty-five, were making their way across Canada. It was not out of the ordinary to see people in their thirties adopting the life style of the highway hippy.

Today there are hitchhikers, but not the hippies of history which has faded into a past culture.

Numbers of hitchhikers has become fewer and fewer on the empty and destitute Trans-Canada Highway of northern Ontario. Media reports of people being murdered along the highway have scared most unseasoned hikers away. During a period of time, there had been four murders committed along a portion of Highway Seventeen. Between an imaginary line between southern Ontario and northern Ontario, starting near Barrie and ending near the lake head of Lake Superior.

Only one of the four victims has been identified to date. One victim was shot point blank in the head and tied to a tree. Two others were shot in the upper portion of the body then left buried in surface type graves. The last of the four victims was not found until the body was to the point of complete decomposition. Was it one murderer or random murders by local people, or transient hippies? No one has been found or charged, evidence is lacking. Someone's loved ones were resting unwillingly near Barrie, Chapleau, White River and Marathon Ontario.

This is not something someone usually thinks about. For someone that has traveled the area and has heard about the murders, well, it ponders the mind at times.

On this particular day, there had not been that many hitchhikers on the highway. Boo guessed that the heat of the day had chased many of them into a cooler location. With the slow paced travel of the truck, Boo took time scanning the sides of the highway. Under trees, fanning their faces with destination cards, hitchhikers waited out the heat of the day. Puffy clouds began to cover the sky like a blanket pulled up to put the day to sleep. Still, the humid heat of the day lingered, creating waves of heat on the hard top that gave objects in the distance a blurry look.

Boo noticed a small figure in the distance, a person of non-description. Obviously this was not a hitchhiker, no hat or heavier coat, no required duffel bag. Whoever it was, was traveling light. As the truck came closer the figure turned out to be a female with only an over-sized handbag on an arm. Short brown hair covered her forehead and tapered over ears, and ended at the base of her head. A lumberjack's plaid shirt hung down covering most of her body. Boo questioned her age when trying to decide if he should stop to offer a ride. Before passing by, Boo quickly struggled to decide. Salami was sleeping in the back. It would not hurt to stop, as long as no big dude jumped out of the ditch. She looked in need of assistance, so, Boo made a decision.

The truck slowed to a stop on the soft graveled shoulder just past the girl. There was an expression of indifference before she slowly turned her head to look at the stopping truck. Boo turned his head to see if she was coming, she seemed to be investigating the situation. Taking her time, she walked to the passenger window and looked at Boo with street wise eyes. There was no need to exchange words, the eye inspection satisfied her, she opened the door and climbed onto the seat.

Boo was a little taken a-back, she did not ask where he was heading or if he was traveling alone. If one was to feel like a fool, it was Boo, she sensed that he was staring at her. With a motion of a hand, she indicated for Boo to move on. Thinking that maybe he was the one making a mistake, Boo put the truck in gear and eased off of the soft shoulder. Maybe she was more of a threat to Boo than he was to her.

Just the look in her eyes reflected the attitude of, 'I do not give a shit about life, I do what the hell I want and to hell with everyone else'. Leaning back in the seat, she placed both legs up on the dash of the truck to revel well tanned legs leading up to skimpy jean shorts. After throwing the over-sized bag onto the floor, she undid the front of the plaid shirt.

Boo tried to break the silence, but questions were repelled by her own questions. "Where are you heading?"

"Where are you heading?" She responded quickly.

"Ah, I am heading west. I have no particular destination in mind," was Boo's answer, but his question was still unanswered.

"That is good enough for me," She answered as if any ramifications of life were of little importance. "I was heading that way anyway."

"I do not even know you, you do not know me," Boo tried to straighten out the implications of her statement. "You just can not decide to travel wherever, with whomever picks you up."

Bull-headed was a good implication of her attitude of life, and of the way she pushed through the days of living.

"Why not, you are heading nowhere in particular, so what is the difference?"

"Are you running away from home, from a boyfriend, your mother?" Obviously, Boo was becoming concerned. "You do not look all that old."

She straightened up at Boo's question. "I am eighteen, and old enough to be on my own." said through a mouth that was chewing on a stick of gum. The way she was chewing the gum showed no signs of finesse, meaning she was not showing maturity.

Boo was becoming worried, being in her presence could become troublesome. Moisture was building between hands and the steering wheel. "Look, whatever your name is, where can I drop you off?"

She asked calmly, "What day is it?"

"I do not know. Now what does that have to do with your name?" Boo's voice raised.

"It depends on what day it is."

"Do not give me that multiple personality bit." No one spoke, Boo opened the vent window to receive cool air. With silent frustration, Boo gave in. "It is Thursday."

"Janis, today my name is Janis, after Janis Joplin. Janis was wild and free, she traveled where and with whomever she wanted."

Boo answered to himself, "Why not!"

"She was a woman that lived life like a man."

"She lived life alright, but where did it take her. Man, she is dead. Janis sure did not hang around in life for very long. I doubt she even remembered enjoying life before an unremembered high ended her life. Do you plan to go out in a flash of fire too?"

"What is it to you?" Her voice sounded mean, she was not getting her way. "You ain't my old-man. If I want my name to be Janis, then it will be Janis, or I will change it when I want."

"What is it going to be on a Friday night, Xavier, the Happy Hooker. What about Sunday, is it going to be the little Virgin Mary."

Boo had hit a tender spot, and there was no way of repelling her slaps. Her hands slapped about his head and she yelled into his ear, catching him off guard, "Who in the hell do you think you are?"

The truck swerved on the highway, Salami never felt a thing as he continued to sleep. Grabbing her slightly opened shirt, Boo forced her off of him and held her back at a distance.

"Look," said a nervous Boo. "I just want to know your name, and where you are heading, okay. That is all, just name and destination." Boo noticed the city limits sign of Marathon.

The girl was now becoming silent, she sat back and adjusted the front of her shirt. "Just the next town."

Boo thought and answered before he had time to change his mind, "No way, you are getting out in this town. You look like trouble to me."

Suddenly both became nervous when they noticed a speed trap. Boo eyed the speedometer, he was not speeding. As if a plan was made long ago in her head, the so called Janis bounced over close to Boo and forced the truck's gas pedal down with both of her feet. Boo concentrated on driving, he was unable to remove her feet. The speed trap cop was sure to notice the haste and the erratic sway of the truck.

Sirens blared in the stillness of the evening. Salami raised his head to look out the window at the flashing lights, but then turned over and went back to sleep with a heavy snore. The highway was not wide enough as gravel sprayed in all directions from the revolving tires.

"You are nuts," Boo mumbled through clenched teeth, as he gained control of the high-speed truck. "Ninety-five is not my idea of a Sunday drive."

Even at the high rate of speed of the truck, Boo's thoughts were clear. Why did she want to go to the next town, why was she at the east end of town instead of the west end leading out of town? She wanted to avoid this town, yet she was heading directly through town.

Salami rolled with the flow of the truck as it made its way through the centre of town. Traffic quickly took to the side of the street, others came to a dead stop. It was not until Boo, his sleeping buddy and this hitchhiker were through the main section of town, when the cop car was able to edge its way in front of the speeding truck.

Boo managed to push the crazed girl away then planted both feet to the brake peddle. With a jerk and a sway, body metal creaked before shaking to a stop on the pavement's edge. The co and car did not seem so lucky, as the braking tires slid on the loose gravel then teetered to a stop on the gravel embankment.

In the distance, other sirens could be heard arriving. "That is great!" Boo said unpleasantly. He looked sternly at the culprit of this situation. "What the hell is wrong with you?"

She sat there, with arms folded, and stared out of the window into the night's darkness. No answer replied to Boo's question, she sat there calm and innocent. Boo threw up arms in disbelief as to what was transpiring. To wait for the cops to arrive, to figure out the situation, was the only logical thing to do.

Shaking mud from his dress shoes, the cop adjusted a gun belt as he climbed the embankment. A Barny Fife he was as he cautiously walked towards the truck. An itching hand hovered over a holstered pistol. On each step, loose gravel adhered to muddy shoes, he shook each leg like a wet dog would do. Boy, he was ready to slap leather. High noon on a darkened highway somewhere in northern Ontario.

Boo forced a smile and showed empty hands over the steering wheel. Something just was not going right, it could only get worse. A feeling of repeating a flawed scene in life over again.

"Okay, keep those hands up, get out of the truck real nice and slow," crackled the cops voice.

Boo made the mistake of reaching down for the door handle. Quickly the cop drew the issued pistol, and pointed the black barrel towards Boo.

"That is far enough, keep those hands up where I can see them, now get out of the truck," said the voice with a bit more confidence.

Boo forced another smile. Into space stared the girl, sitting in the passenger seat. "I can not officer."

"Why not?" Lowering his pistol, his eyes squinted over the pistol's hammer head.

"I hope he blows your head off!" Only her lips moved.

"Do not give him any ideas, he does not seem bright enough as it is," Boo said through smiling lips. Leaning to the open window, Boo raised his voice, "The door will not open by its self, unless I lower my hand to pull the handle."

Into the light of headlights, two other cops entered the situation in progress. Surely they had heard the ongoing conversation. A Sargent spoke up with authority, "I think you had better let him do it Mahony, or we will be here all night. The door will not open by its self." The third cop turned to hide an awkward laugh.

Mahony shook a muddy dress shoe, while reluctantly lowering the pistol. "He looks a little . . .,"

"Ah, put the gun away Mahony, I do not think it is necessary."

"Right Sargent. Okay, you can open the door, but no sudden movements, I have this gun ready." Mahony shook his leg.

Boo stepped from the truck with both hands reaching for the heavens. The though of a gunslinger made him more nervous than the trouble the girl passenger was causing. Shaking their heads, the Sargent and the third cop stood in disbelief of the fear Mahony had caused.

"You are fast on the draw, eh Mahony?"

"Cut the chatter Baker," mumbled the Sargent to his companion. Walking towards the truck with hands on hips, the Sargent took over the situation. Without an explanation, the Sargent stepped to the open door and peered into the yellow light of the cab. "Not again Miss. Evens. Why is it, that this happens when I am on shift?"

Boo had missed something, the simple logic of how the girl's mind worked. She was running away and had done it before, and had been caught, again. "Sargent?" Boo tried to ask of an irritated man giving out more orders.

"Mahony, no, Baker, you take this truck to the station. Mahony, you take this guy. What is your name?"

"Boo!" answered on top of the Sargent's last word.

The Sargent looked sternly for a moment as if pondering Boo's honesty. "Yeah, Mahony, take this guy and Miss. Evens to the station."

Mahony followed the Sargent, attempting to say something in a quiet voice.

"What is it now Mahony? Speak up."

"Ah, Sargent, my car is over there, it is kind of down in the ditch." Mahony pointed into the darkness.

Clutching the middle of an oversized belly, the Sargent turned to face Mahony. "You are giving me a pain, Mahony." Taking a deep breath before continuing in a slow speech. "Take my car, and for heavens sake, and for the sake of the tax payers of this community, be careful!"

Baker and the Sargent got into Boo's truck and headed back towards town. Salami must have been knocked unconscious, or hit his head on the side of the truck during the high-speed chase. He was dead to the world in peaceful slumber.

Mahony gathered Miss Evens by the arm and gently helped her into the police car. With a motion of his head, Mahony directed Boo to get into the other side of the car. Lights flashed and the siren cut hotly through the cool night air, Mahony wheeled the car onto the blacktop. Suddenly a loud voice crackled through the night like a booming fog horn.

"Mahony, I want quiet," Sarge spoke into a chest mounted radio. "Do you understand?" It was obvious in the tone of the Sargent's voice that he was clutching a growling belly.

Instant silence prevailed, Mahony and passengers traveled the deserted streets towards the O.P.P station.

Boo leaned towards Miss Evens to ask, "How is it that all the cops know who you are, and of your many attempts at departing this fair town?" Boo frowned, his brown eyes giving a disdainful stare. "What kind of trouble are you getting me into?"

Before Miss. Evens could answer, Mahony started to give them their rights, which Boo thought should have been given earlier. "You have the right to have an attorney present during questioning, if you wave those rights . . .,"

Miss. Evens in an un-lady-like manner told Mahony off, "Shove it, you clod! Stop playing a cop!"

Mahony paid no attention, as he carried on with the rendition of one's rights. Boo sat back more confused than ever. Enjoying the ride to jail, in peaceful quiet, suited Boo, at this moment. Maybe a good meal was waiting. They do feed prisoners. Salami would be out of luck, unless Mahony arrested him for snoring during a police chase.

Sure enough, as Mahony entered the police station parking lot, he turned on the roof's flashing lights. The Sargent spoke to Baker in a low scornful voice. "I just do not know what to do with this guy, he is getting on my nerves, he is giving me an ulcer."

Baker remover the truck's keys and locked the doors then walked away from the back parking lot where the truck was safe. If and when Salami woke up, he sure will be surprised if not bewildered.

Mahony lead the prisoners to a small room in the brand-new O.P.P station. "You two stay right here, and no talking, I will be right outside of this door."

"Oh, good," trembled Miss Evens' voice sarcastically.

Fresh paint smell lingered, white tiled flooring reflected a shine. The doors and desks were new, no scratches. Paint drop cloths, paint cans, and coveralls rested stacked in the corner. Boo thought for a moment then turned to look at the backs of the wooden chairs they sat in, wondering if are they were freshly painted. After meeting Mahony, Boo wondered about the sanity of the rest of the people in this town.

Boo and Miss. Evens sat there without an exchange of a single word. Her outlook on life did not seem to change, she sat there with legs out-stretched, chewing on fingernail ends and spitting them across the room. Boo rubbed a thigh which was throbbing with the sensation of wounds. Remembering back, he recalled Miss. Evens' fingernails sinking into his flesh as she stepped on the gas pedal.

"Miss Evens," the Sargent said. "The chief will see you now."

"Sargent," Boo called out as the Sargent was backing out of the door. "What about me? I would like to know what is going on."

After pressing a thumb under a lower rib, the Sargent replied, "The Chief will see you next, hang onto your hat, Mr. . . ., whatever your name is." One look at Mahony standing at the door was enough to make the Sargent waddle away in pain.

Baker entered the small room, asking for Boo's drivers licence. It was normal routine, so Boo thought nothing of it at the time. Boo had nothing to hide, had he?

The police Chief, sitting in his office chair looked domineering, tall with hardened features, and a clean chiseled face. Folded together on the desk pad, his hands looked huge, hands that could crush a man. In such a man could there be a soft spot under the cloak of sternness. This job of policing demanded firmness, which his outer features confirmed.

With hands motionless, the chief waited for a knock on the door. When it came, he answered in a firm but soft voice. "Enter." Through the opening door, the Sargent lead Miss. Evens in by the arm. "Thank you Sargent, that will be all."

Standing there, with an air of rebellion, Miss. Evens' eyes floated around the room without observing anything of importance. The Chief stared directly into the young girl's eyes.

"Why do you do this all of the time. Marie, look at me when I talk to you." his voice a tone above normal.

Marie raised her head and looked at the Chief with unconcerned empty eyes. Her hair was a mess, and her shirt was still roughly open from the altercation between herself and Boo in the truck earlier.

"Answer me when I ask you a question. I want to know what you are thinking about under that facade. What is going on in your head?"

"Father, I want to get out of this town." Marie moved to the nearest chair and sat down. "This town is boring," she said, opening the hand bag to withdraw a stick of gum. An open mouth gum-smacking began.

The Chief did not seem pleased with her attitude. "Sit up straight and button up your shirt."

"See Dad, you are always on my case, you never let me do what I want." A bubble cracked between her teeth.

There they were, as they had been before, with the same differences and the same defenses. Lowering his head a little under the burdens of thoughts, the Chief began to reason. "If you do not like it here in our quiet little town, run away. This time try hitchhiking from the west end. When someone picks you up, you will not be coming straight through town where my fellow police officers have orders to haul you home."

"This town needs a little excitement," Marie said while fumbling with the buttons of her Father's hunting shirt. "At lest I bring a little stimulation to this place."

"What about the people that end up in my office. High speed chases, you might cause an accident, someone might wind up dead." Rubbing his eyes with the backs of hands, the Chief contemplated an ultimatum. This was the last straw. Now was the time and place to set things straight once and for all. "Young lady," he said. "We will be here in this office until we come to an understanding, a mutual agreement. No one leaves until you are satisfied, and I am satisfied."

Boo waited while the time passed on the clock's face, his butt ached from the prolonged sitting. Stretching his legs, Boo peered out through the windowed door. 'Yup, Mahony is still there guarding a ruthless criminal.' Boo counted the officers that he could see other than Mahony. Baker was talking to an officer at the front desk, the Sargent was taking an antacid tablet with water, and the Chief was in his office with Miss. Evens. Baker was taking his time with Boo's licence, he spent quite a long time talking on the telephone. After sitting back down, Boo thought about the return of his licence when they let him go. Thoughts of escape entered Boo's mind, he needed a back up plan just in case. A long night being cooped up was not what Boo had planed on.

There was no swaying of the truck comparable to the rocking of a cradle. Salami awoke with a start to the strange feeling of motionless movement. Looking out of the cap's back window, Salami looked at unfamiliar landscape, he looked into the front of the truck, Boo was not there. Shaking his head as if maybe he was still sleeping, but when he opened his eyes the situation was the same, 'Strange', thought Salami. Climbing out over the back tail gate, Salami stretched legs on the still warm asphalt of the back parking lot. Glancing around, Salami noticed bush on three sides and the back of a building doused in flood lights. Walking to the side of the truck, Salami tested the locked doors, while keeping an inquisitive eye on the surroundings. "What the hell."

Sleep was rubbed from eyes, hands itched their way through curly dirty-blonde hair. "Well!" said Salami. "I will have to find Boo to figure this out." Step by step with a turning head, Salami headed towards the back of the building. He began following the brick wall with felling hand towards the front of the building. Salami began to realize the situation when the O.P.P sign came into view. Leaning his back against the wall, Salami relaxed tensed arms. "The fool got caught for that stunt in Wawa. Shit has happened," he said with a laugh at the ironic similarities of the two incidents.

It was past twelve according to Salami's watch, the night was dark and quiet. Standing there for several minutes, it was obvious that a variety of ideas and vague thoughts were going through Salami's head. "Maybe it was simple speeding. I walk in cool and calm, pay the fine and then we are out of there." This was Salami's plan.

Baker had just called the desk officer into the radio room when Salami sauntered into the building towards the front desk. "Tom come and listen to this," said Baker.

"I will be with you in a moment," the officer said to Salami before turning to enter the radio room.

Like radar, Salami's ears listened to every noise. Words echoed off the hollow walls in the station. Baker took off the headset and turned on the external speaker. Salami leaned onto the edge of the oak trimmed front desk.

"Tom," Baker said. "That guy that Mahony brought in."

"Yeah," replied Tom.

"Well, it seems that his truck fits the description of one wanted in Wawa. Maroon, wood running boards, white cap on the back with a maroon stripe."

Salami's ears perked when he heard the description, he leaned even further trying to hear more.

"The O.P.P detachment in Wawa are looking for two guys traveling in a Ford truck." Baker gave a laugh as he and Officer Tom listened to the dispatch. "The two girls we have at the station gave up free information in exchange for immunity."

"Baker here, what did these two guys do?"

"We conclude that these two girls and the two men painted large goose prints on the highway, painted some road signs, and,"

"What else is there? Baker over."

"They got hold of about a couple of hundred pounds of fresh manure, cow shit to be exact, and piled it in piles on the highway behind the Wawa goose. Cars were sliding all over the place. By mid day the whole place reeked of shit."

"The car wash is sure going to make a clean up," added Tom. Baker nodded with a smile.

The radio crackled further information. "The signs said, 'watch out for falling goose droppings'."

Tom and Baker began to laugh, thinking of the mess their counter parts in Wawa had to get cleaned up. "Shit happens."

As the laughter in the radio room climaxed, Salami backed out of the front office. Salami had to find Boo, then find a way out of this place. Lifting his shirt collar, Salami eyed the surroundings to make sure no-one noticed his departure. At the back of the building, a nervous Salami hurriedly began to devise an escape plan. Brain waves began turning gears in Salami's disorientated mind.

Tom cut the laughter to silence in the radio room when he said to Baker, "Do you think we should tell the Chief about this guy we have in the lunch room?"

"He is still in his office, talking to his daughter," laughed Baker. "There is probably enough shit flying in there as it is. He would not believe us, two officers unable to keep a straight face."

Tom pointed to the radio. "Tell the clean up crew in Wawa that we have a vehicle that fits their description." Baker nodded in reply.

From the bursts of dialogue to the moments of silence, it was obvious that the Chief and his daughter had not reached a truce. The Sargent shook his head after pausing at the Chief's door to listen, he then walked away. A police Chief has to be set in his ways, follow the book. Marie had emulated her father's stubbornness, she was determined to have her way, at whatever expense. From the pitch of the female voice coming through the office door, Marie was making the most of the situation, she felt she was on the way in having the outcome lean in her favor.

Looking back into the front doors of the police station, Salami noticed some painters tools and overalls stacked by a ladder. 'Maybe the painters had planned to work late,' thought Salami, mouthing the words. 'They just stopped to get a bite to eat before they got back to painting.'

Pondering the situation took a few minutes. Smiling to himself when an idea struck, Salami glanced twice from the coveralls to the front desk. A plan arrived to get himself and Boo out of this place, and this town. Salami wasted more time checking the outside of the building, inside of the building, the front area, and doors to make sure all was clear of obstacles and police bodies.

Why Salami did things the way he did, no-one knew. Maybe, it was the way he was raised, his mother always asking him if he remembered to do this or that, or if he had forgotten something. There beneath the lights in front of the glass doors, Salami pretended to get into coveralls, stuff another one into the coveralls and place a hat low over his forehead. Not once, but twice, he went through a pantomime of dressing into coveralls before attempting to dress.

Tom emerged from the radio room to take a seat at the front desk. At that same moment, Salami picked up a paint can and walked slouched to the front of the desk. Leaning over the desk to try and see the painter's face, Tom wiped a tear of laughter from his eye. "You did not happen to see a curly blonde haired guy standing at my desk did you?"

Salami shock his head no, as he scratched a cheek with the bristles of a damp paint brush.

"You must be the fifth painter I have seen in here tonight, and there is only one wall painted," noted Tom to the new painter.

Salami's reaction was quick, he replied with a strong slurred Italian accent, "I new here, first time work here ever." A waving paint brush added flare to Salami's imitation of his grandfather, "I paint wall good, you like."

"I wish you could put some colour on the walls instead of plain white." Tom looked the walls over that surrounded the front office and lobby. "Everything is white."

Salami waved the paint brush and shrugged shoulders, over doing his acting. Realizing that he was hamming it up, he made a quick exit down the hallway towards Mahony and the lunch room.

Lowering his head, he dragged a hand along the wall then peeked into the room behind Mahony.

"Mahony," yelled Tom from the front desk. "Leave the painter alone before you create a problem."

Mahony was stopped in his tracks before he was able to interrupt Salami's undercover operation. Stepping back, he rested a hand on the holstered pistol. Before Salami reached for the door handle, Mahony's voice stopped him in his tracks. "No talking to the prisoner, do you understand?"

Again the paint brush waved in the air while Salami over did his acting. "No paint the Prisoner."

Salami entered the lunch room where Boo sat staring at the ceiling. Lifting the brim of his paint cap, Salami grinned a clown face at Boo. "Salami, are you moonlighting as a painter? I would tie your shoe-lace if I were you."

Salami looked down at loose shoe-laces. "No time."

Lifting one foot off of a loose shoe-lace seemed to have corrected the problem. "I thought I would get a job painting while you spend a couple of months in jail."

"What are you talking about?" Boo replied with a half hearted laugh. "It is all that girl's fault. I will be out of here in an hour or so."

"What girl?" Salami looked puzzled, which was not much different than his normal expression. "Never mind the girl. I heard those cops talking out there, something about our girl friends in Wawa, they must have babbled." salami shook the paint brush in Boo's face. "We are wanted men. We Go To Jail. I DO NOT WANT TO GO TO JAIL!"

Boo laughed off Salami's poor acting. "Then we had better fly this coop." Boo realized it was a bad choice of words for Salami. "I mean Escape, we need to escape." Standing, Boo headed for the Door.

Salami pulled back on Boo's shirt. "That guy at the door will not just let you walk out of here." Boo nodded. "Here, put on these coveralls and hat." Salami pulled a pair of coveralls out from it's hiding spot. "I will distract the cop while you sneak out. Take those drop cloths with you."

Boo gathered the drop cloths and held them high to cover most of his face. Salami was to distract Mahony, to allow Boo to pass along the hallway. With paint and a paint brush, Salami headed into the hallway and directly to the wall behind Mahony, where he began to make brush strokes. Boo thought Salami was over doing the paint job with his flare of artistic brush stokes. After a few brushstrokes, Salami called to the Officer.

"Officer, you come here and see if the wall be painted good." came Salami's heavy dialect.

Mahony could not resist being of help. With assurance, he faced the wall then leaned in close to give the job a close inspection. Salami assisted the Officer.

"You stand far back and take a big look over all the wall." Taking the Officer by the arm, Salami lead him back against the far wall, a wall far from the view of the lunch room door. "You see good from here." With assurance, Mahony agreed with the painter.

Boo made his move. Lifting the drop cloths to cover features, he headed out into the front lobby. Leaving Mahony to further inspect the wall, Salami joined Boo at the front desk. Hurriedly, the two began to cover Tom's desk. In the mayhem, Tom payed no attention to the strange faces as he busily gathered paper work into his arms.

A quick escape had to be postponed for a moment. Both escapees fluffed the drop cloths over and over as the Police Chief's daughter left the office. Solid oak slammed against the metal door frame, Marie exited in a puff of smoke. Cussing her way out through the front door seemed logical to her character, Boo had observed. Every Officer there watched the girl make her exit. Salami and Boo copied the same speed of exit.

Taking each an end, the boys fluffed the drop sheet over the desk and over the desk Officer. Mahony waited at the wall for the return of the painter, Tom grabbed for flying papers under the paint cloth. Baker shook his head from side to side, he placed the head set over ears and began to adjust the radio dial.

Once outside, the guys did not see any sign of the departing Miss. Marie Evens. Hastily making their getaway with paint sheets in hands, the boys headed for the back of the parking lot. Realizing something of importance, Boo stopped dead in his track. Salami was more dynamic with his method of stopping, it took a foot stepping on his own loose shoe-lace to halt forward motion. Drop sheets cushioned the sprawling dive.

"What are you stopping for?" Salami picked himself up egging Boo on. "Those cops will be after us in a few minutes. Come on lets move it."

"Salami," Boo asked with a questioning tone. "You would not happen to have the truck keys on you, would you?"

Salami lazily placed hands into the side slits of the coveralls. A blank gaze showed on his face. "It is your truck. Do you not know where your keys are?"

"A vehicle is coming, get behind the truck!" Boo and Salami gathered the drop sheets then hid in the darkness.

Under the parking lot lights, a painter's van stopped at the back door. Seven men in different stages of painter's clothes emerged from the van's doors.

"Follow them," Boo demanded.

As the painters gathered their tools of the trade, Salami and Boo wandered into the commotion and lent a hand bringing paint trays and rollers into the building. A smell of garlic and home made wine vented from the mouths of the men. Good food and wine for supper make men happy and unaware of two extra hands on the job.

Quickly down the hall, past Mahony towards the front lobby, Salami and Boo began to shake and cover the front desk with a drop cloth. Salami placed an end of the drop sheet into Officer Tom's hand and gestured to him to hold it high. Boo ducked under the cover to look for the truck keys.

With antics of an over zealous actor, Salami verbally carried on confusing the Officer. Baker decided to shut the door to the radio room and stay inside, away from the commotion. Mahony still stood facing the wall, deep in thought about the paint Salami had brushed onto it. Real painters began laying sheets down, mixing paints, fixing rollers to wooden handles. No one questioned the presence of extra painters, no-one questioned the different foreign languages being spoken by the painters.

Boo spotted several sets of keys, and grabbed all of them, then made an exit towards the back door. As Salami and Boo made their escape, Tom was left standing holding a painter's drop sheet. Sitting in his office, the Chief never moved, never asked to see Boo.

Scattered between the back door and their mode of transportation, Salami and Boo discarded their hats, coveralls and paint brushes along the parking lot. Without the glare of the truck's headlights, the truck inched slowly out of the entrance and towards the end of town.

A painter pointed from Mahony to another wall. Being accustomed to taking orders, he moved to the opposite wall and leaned back against it. "Now what?" asked Mahony of the painter who said something foreign and pointed down the hall. "Okay I am going."

Watching the Officer walk away, the painter could only shake his head at what he saw. White paint covered the back of Mahony's blue shirt.

Leaving his office, the Chief seemed distraught with a weight on his shoulders making him slouch. A do not bother me look prevailed on his face. Mahony had just peered through the window of the lunch room and noticed his prisoner missing. Turning to faced the Chief, the Chief's tone cut Mahony's words short. "I do not want to hear about any insignificant problem you may have Mahony. Take care of it yourself." The Chief did not look up. "I will be in tomorrow at seven. Whatever you must tell me can wait until then. Good night."

Once Boo and Salami had the truck back onto the main highway, Boo accelerated beyond the speed limit. It was a matter of putting as much distance between them and the likes of Mahony. Boo was wiping perspiration from his forehead when Salami noticed a darkened figure on the side of the highway. They were only about a mile from town and not far enough from the troubles of the night.

"Hey Boo, a female hitchhiker, a girl," Salami beamed with excitement in his voice "I think she needs a ride. Stop, and I will see if I can be of assistance."

"No way!" faltered Boo's voice. "That is the Police Chief's daughter!"

Wind from the speeding truck created little swirling tornadoes that picked up dust from the gravel shoulder along the highway. Once past the lone figure standing there, the truck left the girl choking in the dussty wake. A disappointed face of Salami turned to see a slim shaped arm extend a hand with an unturned finger.

Salami's lower jaw dropped open. "That sweet looking, shapely figure is the Police Chief's daughter."

"Yeah!"

CHAPTER 5
UPRISING

Taking turns at the wheel, Salami and Boo were determined to put as much distance between them and the troubles of Wawa and the Police Chief's daughter. Minutes turned into unnumbered hours of no food, less sleep and sticky sweat clinging to their bodies. By now every Police station along the Trans-Canada highway had been informed of Boo and Salami's escapades. Physical features of them, and a truck description surely had made the daily Police spread sheets; 'Wanted in Wawa for spreading shit around. Wanted for attempted abduction of a Police Chief's daughter, and escaping Police custody.'

Boo dreamed in a conscious manner as the truck rolled down the last rough mountains of the Cambrian Shield. That day in the Steel Mill when he had belted the shift foreman, he had decided to get away from authority, get away from the demands of people. Now, he had brought upon himself more troubles, more pressures, more need to put distance between liabilities and . . ., what was Boo searching for, what was he really trying to escape from?

Salami had taken the wheel while Boo dozed in a fitful slumber. Thunder bay was passed through during the night. Under the rising sun of a welcomed new day, Salami had determined that they were heading slightly north towards Dryden Ontario. A sweaty hand combed through dry tangled blonde hair. 'We sure could use a good clean up,' thought Salami. 'We stink.'

Heavy eyelids twitched while past visions replayed themselves through Boo's mind. Was it an indication of an unresolved conflict back at All Steel. Are there events taking place this very moment, events regarding Boo.

False light filtered into Reese's office, light that was dim. Reese liked it that way. In Reese's mind, the thought that his injuries were worse in his mind than they were physically, tormented his wellbeing. Most of the burn scars that covered his neck and shoulder had faded. Over the past year, the scars had healed. There were revengeful thoughts in Reese's mind, revenge towards Boo.

Reese sat in the dimness of the office making notes on the work schedule. In his mind, he was on the cast house floor of number four blast furnace a year in the past. Each moment, each event replayed in front of his eyes.

There he stood, near the trough as sparks from the furnace spout shot out melted iron and a slag by-product. Boo sat in the control room doing nothing, not following Reese's orders. Sparks illuminated the darkness of the cast house. Men ran for cover while Reese barked out orders as he fumbled with the clay gun. The clay gun that should have plugged the furnace spout with clay, the first time it was placed in position.

Tommy, from security, had been following a trail of odd accidents that had claimed several lives. This trail had brought him to number four furnace. In his clean cut blue security clothes and blue hard hat, Tommy looked out of place. Tall and skinny, more like an ex basketball player than someone investigating steel mill accidents. Tommy was a man of patience with a relaxed demure, not a man looking for evidence to convict a man of murder.

For the past couple of days, Tommy had been keeping very close tabs on the activities of both Reese and Boo. If there was something that was going to happen, he wanted to be there when it occurred. Today, Tommy was hanging around the number four blast furnace, and after examining the work sheets, had suspected that a conflict might happen today. Those examined work sheets showed that Boo and Reese were to work on the same crew for the afternoon shift.

Ducking around the drill control room on number four, Tommy watched Boo emerge from number six blast furnace. Near the trough, Tommy saw Reese walking out of the shadows to face Boo. The cigar that Reese usually chomped on was gone, Reese stood as close to Boo as he possibly could. Boo stood much taller than Reese, his chin only reaching to Boo's chest. Reese spoke quickly and forcefully, hoping to intimidate Boo.

"Tonight's the night we have it out, you son of a bitch," Reese yelled. There was an unprecedented anger in Reese's voice as he stared coldly at Boo. "After the first cast is over, it is you and me in the electrical room. Only the winner is going to come out alive."

Reese disappeared into the shadows as quickly as he had appeared. Only the thunderous roar of the furnace filled the air as Boo stood there with Reese's words ringing in ears. Boo stood alone for a moment then proceeded to walk to the office to check the work sheets. Having done so, he headed towards the locker room. Boo did not seem to be particularly bothered by anything that Reese had said, he knew that in a fair fight it would be himself that would emerge a winner. Yet, he also knew that at no time could Reese ever be trusted to fight a fair fight.

The level of chatter increased as men of different proportions milled around the locker room. Men clad only in towels walked to and from the showers. As the number of men increased so did the chatter. For about an hour and a half, between the three to eleven shift and the eleven to seven shift, the room full of bodies seemed to be in a state of chaos. In a short period of time, the aisles would be empty and the lockers would be silent. But for now, the smell of human sweat filled the air. In a short while the men would be heading home or to their jobs.

As the last man left the welfare room, only silence remained. A cool September wind blew through the open windows above the lockers. It would not be long before the impending Winter would bring its cold blast of arctic air. The summer was eventful, but as the fall of 1979 arrived, and it was obvious that events had changed. The times would never be the same again. Frog was dead, Ziggy was mangled, two friends gone. Victims of industrial accidents.

A stream of light filled with dirt beamed down upon the shoulders of a lone man sitting silently on a hard bench, worn with age and use. Dressed in work clothes, with boot laces untied, his eyes glanced at the concrete floor. He reflected on a different place, a different time. Raising his head, an expressionless face glanced from locker to locker. Eyes seemed to anticipate something that was there, but was not. Closing eyes, he gently rested a heavy head back against the locker.

Long-ish brown hair, cut in a shag style, rested on the shoulders of a six-foot-one-inch body. Boo weighed about a hundred and seventy pounds. His clean-cut face and deep brown eyes were accented by a moustache which extended down to the corner of the lower lip. An aurora around him gave a sense of a man alone, a loner. Boo sat alone with hands resting on his lap, facing upward in a questioning manner. He opened glossy wet eyes and scanned the entire length of the lockers. The sweat of the men was beginning to dissipate. A smile came to his lips, but faded as quickly as it had arrived. Thoughts seemed to depart from his body. No-longer were there lockers or the clanking from the steel mill.

Lowering eyes, Boo bowed his head downward. Above, a beam of light rested gently on slumped shoulders. Sitting on the green painted bench, Boo felt the cool September wind whispering above. Clothes moved in rhythm with the wind blowing gently above the lockers. Around, empty lockers stood waiting to be occupied.

There was a time before this, a good time. Boo's thoughts gravitated towards those times as the wind above caressed the darkening night sky. He wished for the wind to carry him away.

Boo checked the torpedo shaped clay gun, as he stepped onto the cast house floor. This was the clay gun that he was assigned to take care of. After the cast was over, the gun would be swung into the trough and placed at the spout where the molten iron flowed. Inside of the clay gun, heat drying clay would be forced into the hole until the furnace was sealed. Boo's job was to fill the gun after each cast.

With a steel bar in hand, Boo poked at the spout of the clay gun until the hardened clay fell clear of it's opening. Boo tested the plunger as the remaining clay was forced out. Opening the back lid, Boo broke into it's cavity several chunks of clay. Pressing the plunger forced the clay to the front of the spout. Normally the gun would consume about twenty chunks of clay, Boo had placed three into it's chamber. At the lid, Boo shoved one more chunk of clay into it's opening and packed it so that it would remain there, he then locked the lid shut. At the controls, Boo moved the plunger to it's most forward position. Now the clay gun was ready for the cast.

Placing on an asbestos jacket, Boo sat on a bench to wait for the rest of the workers to get ready for the cast. Minutes later Reese walked out onto the cast house floor.

"Cast time," yelled Reese, then took a position off to the side, near where Boo and the drill operator sat. "Let's go Tony."

Tony approached the controls to start the air drill. Within seconds, sparks started to fly, sending a shower of colours out over the cast house floor. Reese paced back and forth as the cast continued. At every twist and turn, he would see Boo's grinning face sending shivers up and down his spine. Reaching for a cigar, he shoved it into a gapping mouth, and started to chew on it. It did not seem to calm the nervousness that he was feeling.

Noticing a motion from Reese, Boo adjusted the position of the last iron torpedo by a remote control lever. Reese was under the impression that Boo would most certainly decline any order that he gave.

The last of the slag spurted from the hole in the furnace, behind it new forming iron spewed forth. Casting was almost over, and Reese thought about the meeting that was soon to take place in the electrical room, between himself and Boo. Reese had everything planned down to a tee this time. In the darkness of the room, Reese's brown nose'ers waited anxiously to use their rubber hoses as weapons on an unsuspecting Boo.

"Plugger up," yelled Reese above the roaring of the starving furnace. With a hand, he directed Tony to lower the clay gun into the trough. Seeing the downward motion of Reese's hand, the operator pressed the plunger button that would force clay into the furnace hole.

Boo sat motionless on the bench.

"Plugger up, plugger up," Reese yelled repeatedly while crimson red iron oozed freely from the furnace. "Plug up the dam thing!"

A devilish grin came to Boo's lips. From across the cast house floor, Tommy Jenkins watched the commotion.

"Pull it back out," yelled Reese to the operator. "The tip of the clay gun is melting. Refill it and try again!" Reese looked around for the clay-man that was suppose to pull the release chain to let the operator draw back the gun. "Pull the dam chain Boo." Boo just grinned at the fuming Reese. "Boo, you bastard!"

Globs of melting cast iron fell from the clay gun's nozzle. Reese pulled several times before the catch released the gun. Unexpectedly, the iron exploded in the hole. No one was safe in the open cast house floor. Tommy dropped to the floor as sparks shot over him. Boo grinned like a Cheshire cat as the sparks exploded wonderfully past the opening. Unlike others, he was protected by safety glass of the operator's room. Tommy shielded himself and listened to the shrill of the emergency sirens blaring as everyone evacuated the area. Tommy counted heads and found that only one was missing, he could see Boo on the far side of the trough, but where was Reese.

Was it an accident? Had Boo something to do with it? These questions raced through Tommy's mind. He had witnessed the whole thing, he had not seen anything out of the ordinary. Most of his suspicions and evidence was melting away. 'Was Boo the only survivor of the conflict between Reese and Boo.' thought Tommy, as he tried to deal with the aftermath of the explosion.

A light flickered on the control panel behind Reese's desk. Suddenly he was back to reality and to his senses. Reese looked up from the scribbling of notes he had been making. From deep inside of emotions, to the outer layer of skin, a chill of death covered Reese's body. He had survived, escaped the clutches of death's retriever.

When the furnace exploded, Reese felt the heat of molten iron burning through the asbestos coat he wore. Sizzling skin, his own sizzling skin; Reese smelt his flesh burning. From the force of the blast, he was knocked to the floor. Suddenly the sensation of falling occurred. Reese fell through a port-hole in the cast house floor used to fill the torpedo with molten iron.

Luck, had it been luck? Reese knew that Boo had failed to fill the clay gun, and its lack of use lead to the excess of molten iron exploding. But the port-hole, below the port-hole should have been a railcar torpedo ready to collect the flowing iron. Reese recalled that Boo had remotely moved the torpedo. Luck for Reese or a mistake by Boo.

Tommy Jenkin's report called it an accident, Reese felt differently. Scars, and a year of therapy convinced Reese that Boo had attempted to kill him. Reese sucked Back on the soggy cigar. From the cast house floor a new cast had begun, Reese knew the sounds, sounds that still shocked nerves.

"Reese, Reese are you busy," call out Jack Miller, as he entered the office. "Reese."

Reese wiped a cold sweat from his forehead with a slap of a hand. "What, yeah, what?"

"Reese, it is me Jack," said the man with a concerned voice. "You look like shit . . ., I mean." Jack caught himself abruptly, trying not to refer to Reese's burn scars. "I mean you are sweating."

A pudgy, grumpy looking Reese spat juice from the end of the cigar onto the floor. "I caught a little fever, nothing serious," said Reese, at the same time turning up his shirt collar to hide the scars. Scars that only he thought were hideous.

"Am I bothering you?"

"Get to the point Jack, I ain't got the time to listen to you beat around the bush about nothing."

Jack sat misshaped hind quarters on the corner of Reese's desk. Pushing back his green hard hat from a warm forehead, Jack scratched a receding hair line. "I hear you were asking questions about Boo."

"Yeah, I was, after rumors got around about the little altercation you and he had." Reese puffed hard on the soggy cigar. "He left you crying on the floor like a baby looking for a mother's tit."

"It was not like that . . ., I . . .,"

"Get to the point." Reese stood quickly, kicking the chair against the control panel. "Tell me what you have to say."

Jack recoiled from his sitting position. "You told me you wanted to get back at Boo."

"I want to hurt him."

"Yeah, well I know you are taking a vacation."

"So, what is it to you?" Reese was becoming agitated, he scratched an itch on the scared skin of his left shoulder. "So, I am taking a vacation."

Jack hesitated, then got to the point, "Boo's friend Salami called home telling his Mother where he is. Salami and Boo are traveling west, taking their time and visiting the sights." Jack took a quick breath. "You are heading to visit relatives out west. I can inform you where Boo and Salami are."

"You can inform me." Sitting back down, Reese squashed the end of the cigar into the desk top. "Inform me how?"

"By telephone, every time Salami's Mother tells my chum's wife, they are neighbors. It is a sure thing. You will be able to track them down."

Reese spat out gray tobacco juice. With a continuing nod, his mind began making plans. Reese grunted. 'A chance to track Boo without him knowing. This family vacation would be a perfect cover.' "I will call you every day if that is what it takes. You had better have information."

Jack Miller backed slightly away. "I will, I would like to see Boo hurt, hurt bad."

"Hurt, he will be hurt." Jack watched Reese softly rub the scared skin on his neck. "I will hurt him."

With a flash of impending peril, Boo awoke to rock music playing on the truck's radio. Early morning light began to heat up the truck's dash board. Boo felt the heat waves rising in his face. Salami bobbed and shook to the music, lost in his own mind's world.

"Boo, are you are awake?"

"Yeah. Where are we?"

"On a highway heading west," Salami answered without malice.

Boo looked towards Salami and declined slapping him behind the head, something may come loose. "What is with the slow traffic?"

"The traffic, all of a sudden began to get heavy, moving real slow." Salami gave a friendly honk of the horn with the beat of the playing music.

Just as sudden, the traffic came to a complete stop, no vehicle was moving ahead. The on-coming traffic lane was clear, not a vehicle in sight.

"What the hell," Salami's voice echoed the frustration of stopping. "There must be a woman driver up ahead that can not decide where to go."

"No, there must be an accident. There is no traffic in the other lane." Both strained heads to look over the distance of cars, but to no avail.

"Pass the cars," Boo suggested to Salami. "Maybe we can find a way around the pile-up."

"Sounds good, all they can do is stop us." Salami cranked the steering wheel over, the truck moved into the opposite lane. "Clear highway ahead Boo."

Salami had spoken too soon. Up ahead the familiar sight of police blue caught their eyes. "It is a road block. They cannot be after us, can they?" Boo asked himself the question.

"We did not do anything that drastic, did we. Like, it was only manure, and you said that girl was only hitchhiking. They do not need all those cops with a big road block." Salami began rubbing sweaty hands around the steering wheel. "What the hell are we going to do now. We can not turn back now, if we do then they will know it is us."

"Hell Salami, run for it. Take that side road running along the highway." Boo pointed as he fastened a seat belt. "Try to bypass the road block. Hell, do not hit anyone."

Salami was not going to question Boo's reasons, he turned the wheel hard to the left onto the dirt road. Dust billowed dryly into clouds behind the advancing truck. "They are sure going to notice us now."

The dirt road, the boys figured, they would use to escape on did not go all that far. Just beyond the road block, the road ended turning back onto the highway. Expecting the cops to follow, Boo turned to see how fast they were moving in an attempt to stop them. To Boo's wonderment, the cops just turned their backs against the onslaught of billowing dust. Blue uniforms turned to light shades of grey.

"Well Salami, I do not think those cops are going to follow us, they are standing there waving their arms at us."

"Boo! Never mind them. Look at what is up ahead," Salami cried out. Clouds of billowing dust passed the truck when Salami applied the brakes. "Native Canadians."

Sure enough, when Boo looked forward, there they were. War paint, bows and arrows, pinto ponies, the whole works. Braves yelled war cries towards them, waved spears and rifles that could go off at anytime. Would they be brave braves ready to attack, or reliving a native ceremony from their past culture.

"We cannot go back, and we cannot go forward."

"Bull-shit Salami! We will out run them. Horses cannot keep up with a speeding truck."

"They have arrows and real rifles that could go off and shoot real bullets!"

"Step on it."

Tires squawked in the loose sand as Salami stepped on the gas pedal. Up onto the highway the truck jerked, Salami steered into the middle of the highway on the yellow lines. Ahead were the horse riders waving their weaponry. With both parties approaching each other the intentions came down to a game of chicken.

"They are not going to let us by, Boo." Sweat beaded on Salami's forehead, he eased up on the gas. "They are heading our way."

"Take to the side of the highway," informed Boo to Salami. Boo clutched the dash and the seat corners.

Bumping along the ditch side of the highway slowed the speed of the truck enough for the warriors to commence a chase. This time the chase involved an all-out attack. Rifles began to discharge into the air, arrows followed through the air in the direction of the boys and their fleeing truck.

"Faster, they are shooting at us." Boo ducked after the echo of a rife shot.

"I cannot go any faster, there are too many ruts. I need to get back onto the highway to gain speed." With one hand on the wheel, the other reached for the radio and turned it louder. "Boo, just don't sit there, shoot back."

'Why not.' thought Boo to himself. Taking a finger and aiming it like a pistol, he cocked a thumb and fired with a verbal sound. "Bang, bang!"

To Boo's surprise two riders and horses fell to the ground with the glory of an old back and white western movie. By what means they fell was not of importance, the score now stood at two for the boys and zero for the pursuers.

"Hey Salami, I got two with one shot," Boo stated in a boastful voice, as he calmly blew imagined smoke from the end of his finger.

"You will have to knock down a few more, I cannot go any faster, I need to get on the highway."

With the horses and riders breathing down their necks, Salami wheeled back onto the highway. A final onslaught of arrows and spears clanked against the metal of the truck. From nowhere an arrow entered the open window and imbedded into the dash board. Salami pressed the gas pedal to the floor. Hot tires griped the heated asphalt. Boo and Salami were making headway, they were placing distance between them and their pursuers. Glancing from each other to the arrow, the boys swallowed with gratitude for their salvation.

"Another road block, Boo," yelled Salami above the rock and roll music of Chuck Berry's rendition of, 'Hot Rod Lincoln'.

"Keep going."

To their surprise, the cops ahead opened the road block to let the fleeing truck through. Both Boo and Salami turned back their heads out of the side windows. Again, they looked at the embedded arrow in the dash, then to each other. Colour slowly returned to their pale faces.

"Hell, that was some Uprising," informed Boo to a shell-shocked buddy.

Backed up traffic gazed in wonderment at the dust covered maroon truck passing by with an assortment of arrows protruding into its shell. Had the truck passed through a time medium, or had they just been in the middle of something they had no right to be in. In life, it is sometimes this same situation that determines the calamities of peoples lives, be it good or bad.

"This is Paul Jakson reporting for C.B.C. radio, bringing to you an update of the day's news.

"News reports confirm that the situation near Dryden Ontario was just an internal conflict of a Canadian Native clan. An elder woman known as Matose had walked to the centre of the demonstration. Without words, she turned and walked away, all the Native people followed her back home. The only casualty of this demonstration, was of an unknown maroon truck heading west with arrows embedded in its body. Police report, that this same truck, being driven by two young men, are being sought for questioning for other incidents that have occurred in Wawa and Marathon Ontario."

Only those listening to the radio had heard the news of the day. Salami ejected a tape and inserted another one, rendering old rock and roll music. Distance between whatever was behind them was of little importance. They had yet to stop to see the added decorations they had picked up. Soon, the low rolling hills of Manitoba would show the beginnings of the prairie grass lands.

CHAPTER 6
FAMILIES

It seemed like a dream, but every now and then, Boo and Salami would glance at each other. The only reminder of the past day were the arrows in the side of the truck and in the front dash. As if scars of honor, Boo decided to leave the arrows where they were, embedded in the truck.

At a gas station on a down slope of the west side of the Manitoba boarder, the boys stretched their legs. Late night rays of the setting sun gave a golden yellow haze to the sky. Boo stuck a finger into a bullet hole in the fender of the truck.

"Ah, you fellas have a run in with a war party or something?" asked the gas station attendant while he inserted the gas nozzle into the truck. "There are quite a few arrows, and a few bullet holes."

"Yup," confirmed Boo.

"Did you shoot back?"

"Yup," assured Boo.

"Would you mind filling the truck up as fast as possible," Salami pressured with a hint of play. "They may still be after us." Salami stretched his neck to look back up the highway in the direction from which they arrived from.

As the truck and the tired guys pulled out of the gas station, they noticed the young attendant peering up the highway. For all they knew, the attendant would spend the rest of the night checking for any advancing war parties.

Taking a turn at the wheel, Boo assumed the early evening drive shift. Salami slouched against the passenger door for a little shut eye. Making it to Winnipeg was the plan before they would feel a little more at ease. Thirst and hunger was becoming prevalent. A quick washup and a change of clothes at the gas station gave a fresh perk-up to their attitudes. Warm prairie wind felt nice flowing through the truck's open windows. Boo kept a slow easy pace, there was no need to attract attention. As if the truck's appearance was not enough to bring inquisitive eyes.

Boo had hoped that the problems they were leaving behind would stay behind. Only the coming days would bring an indication of what was in store for the two friends.

Waking from a dream of American movies, of Cowboys and Indians, Salami questioned Boo. "Where are they, where are we. How far are we from Winnipeg?"

"Should be close. It is now about nine thirty. I figure we should be there about eleven." Boo looked at his wrist for a watch. Remembering that he had thrown it out of the window back at their first rest stop in Wawa, Boo smiled. They no longer had to punch a time clock, so why the need to be governed by time. "Salami, we get there when we get there."

"Boo, I have relatives near Winnipeg, they would be more than pleased to feed us and put us up for the night." Salami looked through one opened eye. "What do you think?"

"Do they have a daughter to go with the food?"

"Sorry Boo, just a son."

"Ain't interested," pondered Boo. "Tell you what, you drop me off down town. I will find some female action, then when you have finished visiting with your relatives come and find me."

"Sounds okay, if that is what you want, thanks."

A glow of city lights could be seen like a glowing dome on the semi-prairie. At every closer mile, the city was still a far distance away. When the heavy night settled over the prairie town, Boo began making his way through the traffic lights of a busy city. At the first main intersection, Boo pulled the truck to the curb and got out. The slamming of the truck door woke Salami from sleep.

"It is all yours Salami," said Boo through the open window. "Just bring it back in one piece." Boo looked at the arrow in the dash. "At lest no worse than it is now." Stepping backwards onto the sidewalk, Boo stiffened when he noticed a group of girls near a display window.

Wiping sleep from eyes, Salami slid over into the driver's seat. Pulling out into the traffic, he waved back. "Take it any way you can Boo. I will pick you up in a few days. Thanks for the wheels."

Salami had a fair idea where he was going, and how to find his relative's home. Like Salami's Mother, his aunt was a first generation in this country. His aunt looked and spoke broken English like his Mother. Unlike his family of only one child, himself, his aunt had ten kids. Frank was the same age as Salami. As he remembered, his cousin was a little bigger in weight.

After an hour of searching, Salami found the house. Words were few when the front door opened. Like a whale swallowing krill,

Salami was swallowed in through the door. Hugs, kisses, food, drink and a bed after a night of family stories. A bed, and sleep followed.

Vacations are the rewards for years of endless days of labour. For most, vacations are spent sipping beer in a reclining chair beneath a shade tree in the back yard. Once-in-a-while, enough money is put aside for that life-time trip. The planning, preparations and those sleepless nights of anticipation unfold. It was drawing near to the time of departure. A family was starting their vacation trip that would take them across western Canada, and up to the coast of British Columbia.

It would be the first trip for Suzie, Al and Mary, the first time in their lives that they would meet other family relatives. It would be the first time a girl in her middle teens would have a life.

"You may be seventeen," Suzie's Mother stated. "But you are not going to wear that skimpy bathing suit on this trip."

"But, Mom! I like it, and all the other girls I know are wearing them."

"Other girls can be seductive, but your Father will not allow you to be seductive," Mrs. Roberts had given a piece of her mind. "The case is closed, put it back on the shelf."

Shopping with her mother, Suzie found boring. Her Mother would never let her do what she felt was good for her. In two days, she would be with relatives on the beaches of Winnipeg Lake, in a 1914 swimsuit. Mrs. Roberts took six-year old Al and Mary by the hand and headed out of the Station Mall's west exit. Suzie thought of Thursday, and the day their trip would take them out of town.

Reese Roberts waited in the Dodge station-wagon, a yellow lemon colour. Out of the side window, Reese spat cigar juice onto the hot pavement. Wet spit sizzled. Reese rubbed the scars on the back of his neck. Looking over the road map of the trip, his thoughts were mostly on seeking out Boo, his nemesis. Tomorrow they would be on the road, as early as he would be able to get the family moving. A family vacation, or a trip to satisfy his vengefulness?

"Hi Dad!" Al called out as the family approached the car.

"Hello Son." Reese began to try and fold the road map. "Dam map."

Suzie grabbed the map and quickly folded it into a clean little package without any difficulty.

"Thinks she is smart eh, Al."

Al looked back at Suzie sitting there with a slight pout on reddish lips. "Uh ha Dad."

As planed, Reese was up early the next morning, herding the family into the packed station-wagon. In the mood that Reese was in, it would not take long to get to Winnipeg. Word, from Jack Miller, was that Salami was at relatives in Winnipeg. Before the early morning rain, Reese hooked up the hard top trailer to the sagging Station-wagon. At six-fifteen the family sped along the highway in hot pursuit of a happy leisure vacation. This family seemed divided on what was to be the ingredients for a happy vacation. Al and Mary slept with heads together, Mrs. Roberts tried to wipe sleep from eyes. Moping in the back seat with ear phones blasting the latest music craze, Suzie dreamt of skimpy bathing suits and boys to ogle after her. With the rain, Reese had an excuse to push the traveling, push straight through to Winnipeg.

"Hey Salami, wake up," called cousin Frank. "Hey, wake up. The better part of the day is over."

Rolling over from a deep restful sleep, Salami looked into the chubby face of his cousin. Rubbing sleep from eyes, that wished for a few more minutes of rest, Salami blocked the brightness of the day.

"It is past noon, the sun is out, it is a hot day, the huge mosquitoes have died, there is wine chilled just waiting to be dispensed of." Frank took a breath that made his large body expand.

"Yeah, okay, noon, I am awake," groaned the dry mouth of Salami. "Where is everyone?"

"They left for the beach at about eight this morning. I think you have had a good enough sleep for a couple of days. It is now party time." Frank's belly shook happily.

Salami wiggled fingers through his curly head of hair, then scratched every other itchy body part. 'That is better,' sighed Salami to himself. 'I need a piss.' Last night's rented wine sat heavily in his lower bladder.

"First, we will have some wine and cheese, then we head to the beach with two ladies I have procured for ourselves," said Frank, lifting baggy, flowered, boxer swimming trunks higher on hips. "Then tonight we will make the rounds of the bars in town."

"Sounds good, but right now, I need to piss real bad."

Frank disappeared into the basement while Salami went to relieve himself of excess wine. No sooner had Salami emerged from the bathroom refreshed, when Frank placed wine and cheese into his hands. With a jug in one hand, and another jug of home-made wine balanced on his shoulder, Frank tipped the jug and swallowed.

"Let's go cousin." Frank motioned Salami to follow.

Cousin Frank tipped the scales at two hundred and thirty pounds. As jolly as his weight, Frank was easy going, ready for any kind of laugh and loved to laugh. Girls somehow favored his humor and style of life, his long jet black wavy hair and blue eyes.

"What happened to your truck," questioned Frank, plucking the feathered end of an arrow.

"It is not my truck, and last night I had thought those arrows were just part of a dream." Wide eyes seemed as impressed as those of cousin Frank. "A war party attacked us, I think."

Frank sipped wine, Salami eased the truck backwards out of the paved driveway of a cozy ranch style house. Wine dripped down Frank's chin beneath smiling lips. Frank's belly jiggled as he laughed blissfully. Pointing in a direction to go, Salami followed the orders.

"So where is your chum?"

"Oh an arrow got him." a cool low modulation came from Salami's mouth.

Frank stopped smiling, his cheek jowls quivered. "Shit!"

After a long pause, Salami began to laugh at the sad look on Frank's face, he did have a sad puppy dog mug. It was no wonder the girls all like him. "No, Boo is just fine, I dropped him off down town last night. He told me to pick him up after I had visited family for a while."

"Whooo . . ," Frank sipped from the jug. "Head up that street, then take a right."

Waiting anxiously at a turn off, at a road leading to a beach, two girls stood waiting for Frank. From a distance, the two blonde girls fit Frank's description of beauty and elegance with slender legs slightly tanned and faces of external beauty.

For Salami, that was enough, he had no long-term ideas. It had been several days that turned out to be weeks when he had last thought about his wife. There had been few times that he had thought about his child. Boo had told him not to give up on them. This tagging along was Salami's idea and his alone.

"There they are Salami, just as I said."

As the truck slowed to a stop, the girls seemed in awe of the porcupine quilled truck. They were a little suspicious until a reassured smile from Frank popped out of the passenger window. There was no hesitation, Frank quickly opened the door to assist them into the truck.

"Ladies, the man I told you about, my cousin Salami. Salami meet Toni and Terri." Frank hugged Toni affectionately. "Twins, I could not break up a set."

Hello's exchanged, the girls stared at the arrow imbedded into the dash. Being polite, they decided not to ask. Onward to the beach headed the foursome as small talk consumed the trip. With the jug of wine making the trip back and forth, slowly Salami's story began to entertain the captive audience.

To all concerned, the four had hit it off well. Sand, wine, the swimming, the food and the rest of the family and friends on the beach stretched the day into early evening. Weather in the nineties, hot sand and water at body temperature whiled away any inhibitions Salami's mind held.

The Roberts pushed the limits of traveling, they drove the day and night through the rain. Reese was determined to out run the bad weather. Getting to Winnipeg before Boo and Salami left town was the driving force behind his excessive driving speed. Once the Roberts family crossed the border into Manitoba the weather changed. With the bright sun rising behind them the heat also climbed into a forthcoming heat wave. Even with the windows opened, and the least amount of clothes on, the sweat poured from their bodies. Twenty hours of non stop driving etched lines of discomfort and anxiety onto their faces.

By evening, the heat was tolerable when they arrived into Winnipeg at about seven o'clock. Reese's brother and family were the first relatives they would meet on their trip. Bob and his family were camped at a beach on the south end of lake Winnipeg. A cool dip in the lake would be of welcome by the drive-weary people.

Almost upon meeting, after the greetings, hugs and kisses, the families sided with those of common interest. Kids bonded with the interest of playing on the sandy beach. Women talked women talk, and the men placed their butts on lounge chairs and opened cooled beers. Suzie was the only one left out of the picture, she was not an adult and not a kid, there were no other family members her age.

It took the rest of the evening, with a good night sleep to calm the jittery travelers. Reese and Bob talked late into the night. Even the next morning, the two resumed their positions on the lounge chairs and sipped beer straight from the bottle. Reese fished for information about the Winnipeg area without really mentioning his injuries and grudge towards Boo. It was obvious to Bob, when Reese mentioned some references, that the end of Reese's cigar became chewed beyond use.

After a short noon-hour nap, Reese and Bob decided to take a walk along the beach with a fresh beer to cool their thirst. Two middle aged men, one short and chubby the other taller and slim, they resembled Mut and Jeff. They took their time walking along the sand, their eyes wandering from one girl's body to another. Their eyes never fell upon the same bathing suit twice.

"Get a load of that one," said Reese spitting cigar juice onto clean white sand. "Nothing but a shoe string."

"Why in hell didn't the girls wear bathing suits like those when we were young?" Bob's eyes followed another beauty as she ran and bounced along the beach.

"Hey Bob, I brought my shotgun, maybe we could get a little trap shooting in before we have to leave."

"Great! There is a range just north of here." Bob tightened both hands around the beer with excitement. "We can take a ride up there after supper."

As they walked, Reese's attention was aroused by some young people coming towards them. It was obvious that Reese had noticed the two young blondes first. The large fellow carrying some jugs was of no interest, but the curly blonde haired guy was too familiar. Reese chewed a large portion of the cigar and spat with force. With an elbow and a motion of his head, Reese beckoned Bob to skirt away from the approaching foursome.

"Hey Salami catch." Frank tossed a gallon of wine over to Salami who had just finished laying out a blanket. "Catch Salami."

Salami fell back onto the blanket beside Terri, and offered the wine to her. With pleasure, Terri sipped from the blue tinted glass jug. Frank, in a playful fashion played the fool by rolling around in the sand, trying to drink by tipping the jug from arms length. Laughter of fun surrounded the four on a beach of many having the same enjoyment of summer.

Reese watched from a distance as Bob questioned him as to what he was staring at. "That guy is a friend of a guy I am looking for. His name is Salami and his friend's name is Boo."

"Well just go up to him and say hi." Bob looked onto the crowed beach. "Which guy is it?"

"I did not say he was a friend." Reese puffed dark smoke from the cigar. "Boo is the guy that caused me to have these scars. If I get my hands on him." Reese crushed the cigar between fat fingers.

Toni rolled around with Frank in the sand, trying to take the wine jug from him. Terri turned to Salami when she noticed two guys looking strangely at them. From the corner of an eye, she watched to confirm that it was them the men were looking at.

"Salami, I think two weird guys are staring at us," Terri stated.

Quickly Salami turned, his eyes drifting from point to point, focusing for a second on many faces in the crowd. "Which guys, where are they?"

When Terri brushed hair from her face to look, the men were gone, faded into the crowd of faceless faces. "I do not see them anymore," said Terri with a whisper.

"I tell you Bob, if I follow this guy Salami around, he will lead me to that bastard, Boo." Spit formed at the corner of Reese's lips. Pulling his tee shirt from a sweating chest, Reese could feel the beating of his heart increase with growing anger.

Bob understood very little of the causes that dictated Reese's scars. The names of Salami and Boo were only names without faces. It was confirmed that Reese detested this guy named Boo. Bob had a feeling within that Reese wanted to hurt, hurt Boo bad. How bad, at this moment, unknown.

"Reese, do you think that Boo is here at the beach?" asked Bob following Reese around to the outhouses set back from the beach.

"He may not be right here. If Salami is here, Boo must be somewhere in Winnipeg." Reese emptied the last mouthful from the beer Bootle then slammed it forcefully onto a picnic table. "He is here in Winnipeg, I know he is."

"What did he do to you?"

"This!" Reese pulled the tee shirt off a shoulder for a brief second then pulled it up to hide the scars. "He did this to me, he dam near killed me. No son-of-a-bitch labourer is going to do this to me, then get off scot-free."

Hate was on Reese's face, hate was in the way he walked away along the beach back to the camp site. "First, we will go back to the camp and get dressed, then head back here to tail Salami back to

Boo." Reese stopped walking, when sensing that Bob was not by his side. "Are you with me?"

Bob acknowledged with a reluctant nod of his head, he quickened a walking pace.

Summer days last longer then cold winter days, hours of sunlight stretch the limits of nine-thirty in the evening. Toni was hooked on Frank, Salami was Frank's cousin, Terri was Toni's twin, so it was logical that Terri fancied Salami. Frank downed the last drop of wine from the jug while the last rays of the setting sun sunk below the horizon. Toni pulled Frank to the ground, kissing and nibbling him behind the ear.

Frank shook like a bowl of Jell-O under the teasing Toni. "I will, I will, anything you say I will do it, stop, stop, no, keep doing it." Laughter searching for a catch of breath giggled from Frank's mouth. Springing onto feet like a rising hot air balloon, Frank began gathering the jugs. "Lets move it, Toni wants a night on the town."

Terri jumped up with excitement. "What Toni wants Terri wants."

Salami whispered hopefully to himself. "I hope she wants what I crave."

Reese and Bob, dressed like tacky undercover cops, were waiting in the parking lot, ready to tail Salami. Reese and Bob sported sneakers and summer coats with sunglasses to hide behind under the darkness of the evening. They were unnoticeably noticeable against the casual attire of the beach going crowd.

When Boo's maroon truck pulled onto the highway, close behind was Bob's green Gremlin, it's motor idling faster then it should. At a safe distance, Reese and Bob followed the truck around town. From the beach to Frank's house, to the girl's house, then to the downtown area of Winnipeg. Lights, cars and people mingled in a festive mood along the entertainment section of town.

"How long are we going to follow these people?" questioned Bob of Reese who sat there puffing relentlessly on a fat foul smelling cigar.

"As long as it takes. Keep your eyes on the truck. Do not let them get out of your sight." Reese clenched hands together. "Until Salami leads me to that son-of-a-bitch. I need to inflict pain upon Boo's body."

Bob's eyes floated with mixed feelings of unanswered questions, and a true lack of commitment to Reese's intentions. Reese was his brother, a domineering brother.

"Frank," asked a slightly lightheaded Salami. "Do you know anyone that drives a green Gremlin?"

Frank swayed his head back and forth in reply. "There are too many little green gremlins in this town."

Arm in arm, the boys lead the girls from the truck to the heavy country sounds of a bar on the city's main street. Reese and Bob pulled the Gremlin into a parking space across the street to wait for an opportunity. For the rest of the evening, Salami put the ghost of the green Gremlin out of thoughts.

After waiting fifteen minutes, Reese decided that the two of them should pay the bar a visit. It was obvious that they stood out from the crowd within the mix of country fashions, Reese and Bob favored old Florida folks. Patrons stared at them as if they were gallery objects from a past forgotten fashion era. The two did not fit in with this clientele. Turned up collars, white sneakers, flowered pants and ladies sunglasses made Reese, a man of anger, feel like an object of ridicule.

"Bob let's wait outside," informed Reese. This little incident fumed an even deeper hatred towards Boo. Bob did not hesitate to retreat.

It was becoming noticeable that Frank was becoming very light-headed from the day long consumption of wine. Salami was not far behind. Both Toni and Terri felt the tingling that made the body feel light and limber. Was it the wine, or the fact that Salami's advances were welcomed by Terri. After a slow dance with Terri, Salami began to kiss her behind the ear as he whispered a verbal advancement.

"Why not take a moonlight drive to a place where we can enjoy the sights." Salami swallowed a dry mouth.

Terri stood up with authority, something that was usually a trait of her sister, and demanded in a voice that grabbed the attention of other patrons. "If we are going to go parking then let's go. I am ready now."

Heads turned, Salami seemed to be taken aback. Toni lifted Frank by the arm coaxing him onto rubbery feet. It was confirmed that the girls were ready to go with or without the boys. Cluing in, both Salami and Frank took a last gulp of their drinks then followed on the tails of their dates.

As casually as possible, the four left the bar through the lobby and the side entrance that led along a lane-way between the buildings to the back parking lot. Frank expanded his chest and breathed in the fresh air of the night.

"Where to now, I am raring to go," his words trailed off, the fresh air made eyes blur, his head felt light. Without assistance, Frank's huge body stiffened and began to lean backwards. "Catch me."

Three friends clung to the heavy frame, but with little support, Frank rested flat on his back on the warm asphalt. Frank laughed, lack of oxygen deprived his brain causing an outburst. "I am okay, I just felt like a little rest," said Frank, between tears of laughter beading at the corner of eyes.

All three strained, Salami grunted in their effort to raise Frank back onto his feet. Upright and somewhat stable, Frank took in slow shallow breaths until the blur faded from his mind.

Delayed laughter from the girls built until Salami joined in, then they laughed at Frank who reciprocated happily.

Reese nudged Bob dozing due to the late hour of the night. "There they go, come on, we will trap them in the lane," informed Reese, as he opened the door and made his way across the street. "Are you behind me, Bob?"

Reese was half way across the busy street before Bob realized that he was suppose to follow. "Okay, Okay, I . . . .." Bob hustled to get his body in motion to follow his brother into the unknown.

Echoes of a voice broke into the laughter of the small group of friends. Words were directed directly towards Salami. Both girls clutched the arms of their partner in reaction to the darkened figure plowing towards them. Frank and Salami faced the two figures that were faceless against the brightness of the street light. No words were uttered by the group, they waited for the next bombardment of profanity.

"Stop, you son-of-a-bitch, I want to talk to you," yelled an aggressive man capable of inflicting pain. "You, yeah you. That is right, it is you I am after."

Salami stepped forward with a clenched fist resting, waiting at belt height. "What can I do for you two guys?"

When Reese and Bob closed the distance, their outfits were the first thing noticed by the four huddled together. Frank, with his brand of humour, commented on the flowered pants held up by wide white belts. "If you guys want to make a living mugging people, I would have selected a slightly less flowery get-up."

Reese's growling voice sounded familiar to Salami. "Watch your lips, fat boy."

Toni held fast to Frank's arm as he edged forward, she could feel the tensing of arm muscles. There was no chance of a civilized conversation, Reese's voice erupted into a shouting match that sent fists into a striking pose.

"I want to know where your friend is?" Reese pointed a short stubby arm and finger towards Salami.

"Friend, my friend?" Salami squinted, trying to see a facial out line that he could recognize. "Who the hell is asking?" Salami could smell the pungent odor of stale cigar smoke in the air.

"Your friend Boo. I want to know where your friend Boo is hiding?" Reese spat dry tobacco juice towards Salami's feet.

Eyes lacking the night vision of a cat, strained to remove the shadows from the strangers standing before them. The taller fellow stood quietly to the side of the loud mouthed rolly-polly man. Salami questioned his own mind, but answers were lost under the influence of wine.

Salami dropped a clenched fist slightly. Who the hell is asking, are you guys cops?"

"Dressed like that, no way!" deduced Frank. "Cops do not dress like fashion-less tourists."

"Frank, I think I know who this fat little fruit-cake is." Salami stretched taller with a build-up of renewed confidence, "Boo and him had a little conflict going on between the," he said with a growing anger in his voice. "That bastard killed a good friend of ours. Frog did not need to die!"

"I want Boo, and I will go through you to get at him," Reese spitted his words with frustration of losing the advantage of anonymity. "Where the hell is he?"

Salami retaliated with a child's voice, "Oh you scare me." Salami toned-down his voice with anger. "I will not tell . . .."

Words had hardly left Salami's lips when a blur of knuckles contacted teeth behind a new tender lip. Salami landed hard against the ground. Small pebbles cut into his back. Lying there bewildered,

Salami stared at the sky, oblique by the water forming in his eyes. Frank reacted within a second, a right-handed swing headed towards Reese's head. Reese ducked the intended punch which then made a cracking sound against Bob's forehead. Bob dropped then rolled into a ball against the red bricked wall.

Wine had taken the stamina from Frank's constitution, he leaned forward without stability. Reese took advantage and applied several quick fists to the jaw portion of Frank's face. Blood puffed within the inner layer of skin on Frank's upper lip. A lower split lip spurted a stream of warm liquid down the chin and onto the neck. Falling lifeless, Frank collapsed to the ground. Toni and Terri guarded their fallen protectors. Fighting the urge to stay down, Salami rose to his feet with both fists cocked.

"Where the hell is Boo?" Reese yelled, while landing several kicks to Salami's chest.

Two piercing screams bounced between the walls of the two buildings lining the lane-way. Reese backed away, he reached for Bob and pulled him to his feet by the scruff of the neck. Both men retreated to the noise and night-commotion of traffic and people. Toni lifted Frank's head and pressed a napkin to his lips. Salami lay cradled in Terri's arms. Because of the wine, the fight seemed like a past memory of inflicted pain occurring at the present time.

Reese turned and yelled from beneath the glow of the street lights, "Tell Boo that I will be after him."

"Cousin, what the hell, who the hell where those two . . ., jerks." Frank spat a glob of blood that tasted sweet on the tongue.

Salami groaned, "I will tell you later. Let's get out of here."

A silence returned to the lane when all parties had left to go their separate ways. Reese and Bob, in their green Gremlin, sped away as if they were the ones being chased. Salami and Frank, comforted by Terri, climbed into the back of the truck. Toni took it unto herself to drive them to the safety of the girl's apartment.

Under the girl's care, the boys were mended and soothed. In the late hours of the night, Salami ventured to tell the story of Boo, the plant, and this guy Reese, who was after Boo. Hours later found the two couples in the comfort of each other's arms, asleep and safe from the events of the early evening.

"How is your head?" asked Reese, as the Gremlin made its way back towards the camp ground. "It ain't bleeding."

"There sure is a bump. It feels as if someone had drilled a hole into my skull."

"Put ice on it when we get back to camp. Bob, tell the wives that you hit your head on the car door." Reese stared straight ahead. Bob noticed a strange anger gripping at the folded lines on Reese's face. A look that Bob did not like, a feeling of doom that he wanted no part of.

"Reese, what have you steaming in your mind." Bob rubbed the bump on his forehead. "How bad do you want to hurt this Boo fellow?"

"Chances are Salami is going to get in touch with Boo. Both of them are heading west. Tonight, our brother-in-law in Medicine Hat is going to receive a phone call." Reese's grip on the steering wheel turned his knuckles white. "Our brother-in-law is the type of guy that will relish in what I have in mind."

Bob decided that he did not want to know anything more of Reese's problems or plans.

Before the sun cracked the edges of the eastern forest, Reese had both families saying their good byes. Reese was on a mission, not a vacation.

"Take care Bob, I will redeem that knot on your head for you." Reese closed the car door against Bob's silence. "Good bye, take care." Reese was now on a direction that would take the family to Medicine Hat Alberta. There, Reese would keep in touch with Jack Miller about the locations that Salami and Boo had been and where they were heading.

Salami moved about with the night's pains, he apologized for his need to depart. A friendship between himself and Boo was important. Salami needed to find Boo before Reese did. Unfortunately, Salami did not have regrets leaving Terri, he found it easy to leave other women, including his wife. Why did he feel a kinship to Boo, a kinship of more importance. Frank, with arms around Toni and Terri, waved sadly at Salami's departure.

CHAPTER 7
SHOTGUN WEDDING

Boo felt that leaving the truck with Salami would not do any harm, hell, there were arrows and bullet holes in it already. As Salami pulled away from the curb, Boo did not look back, his eyes were fixed upon a cluster of girls standing in front of a theater. With Salami off to visit relatives, Boo would do a little visiting with the friendly people of Winnipeg, maybe these young ladies.

"Ladies," Boo bowed slightly. "may I be of assistance. There seems to be a difference of opinion being bantered about."

Of the four girls, three of them smiled when Boo interrupted their conversation. A chubby red-haired girl spoke right up without considering Boo's intentions. "Hi, hello," Boo nodded in response. "you see, three of us want to go to the hotel, any hotel, but she wants to be a party pooper, she would rather see a movie," said the red-haired girl, pointing a disgusted finger at a shy-looking girl with an old fashioned curly hair style. Thoroughly not ugly, she wore long curly hair, set in a ringlet style of the thirties.

Boo smiled towards the girl, she lowered her head with a slight innocence. "I would gather that she is a little opposed to the clientele that these houses of illusions sometimes display."

Several of the girls looked at each other, wondering about the meaning of Boo's statement. Only the shy girl seemed to understand. Eyes looked up from under thin brows, she peeked into Boo's brown eyes then quickly looked away. There was a instant, hidden attraction immediately sensed by both Boo and the curly haired girl.

"I will tell you how I will eliminate this need for further discussion." Boo walked towards the shy girl, extending a hand as a gentleman would. "I shall be your body guard, Miss? May I escort you?"

A glowing smile fought off a frightened heart, she looked at Boo as if he were a Prince Charming, climbing down from a white steed. Slender fingers reached for Boo's callused hand. Dumbfounded girls watched their friend being lead away along the crowded sidewalk. They inquisitively followed like children following a Pied Piper.

From the peacefulness of the farming community surrounding Winnipeg City, these four farm girls descended into a world of sinful nights. Each one seeking to gain the knowledge of the lives that live in the fast lane of life. To dream of being part of the same life for the duration of one night before the rural lives of their families commenced the next morning.

Across the extent of the prairies, the lingering sun's rays diminished as the hour of ten gave way to the neon lights of a city. A sunset of flaring red flames blended into the darkening night sky. Under the veil of darkness, the day's morals are forgotten for the sinful pleasures hidden in the minds of those that dare.

Tonight, was the night, the four girls had decided, to taste the experiences of adventure. What lay before them was a style of life they had never been exposed to. Young people from an easy-going community were seeking the excitement of the fast pace life of city people. Those trapped in chains are held for eternity to a city, they long to escape to the illusion of a country life.

Twenty miles outside of Winnipeg, the morning of this day was like any other morning for an eighteen-year-old farm girl. There were chores to do. Being a girl was not an exception to be excused from honest farm work. Being the oldest of six girls meant having a great portion of responsibilities on one's shoulders. Setting a good example to those younger members of the family was bequeathed to Irene.

Chores must be completed every morning and every night before free time was allotted. Cows to be milked, chickens fed, eggs gathered and house-hold chores all had to be completed. Milking of the cows was almost completed when three female figures entered the barn to sneak up behind Irene, hidden in oversized coveralls.

In unison, the three girls called out in a manly voice, "Hello Irene."

The milk cow twitched in response as Irene squeezed a tit of her udder slightly too aggressively.

"Hello, Irene," greeted the three girls once more. "Are you not finished milking yet?"

"Almost, Zoe," answered Irene while continuing to milk the cow.

In the background the girls gathered; Zoe, a chubby short girl, Jo-Ann, skinny and almost six feet tall, and Sandy, a tomboyish vixen. They carried on several conversations at one time as girls usually do. For the most part of their growing up years, the girls were and had been best friends. Sometimes Irene was left out of the group's outings and adventures. It was not that Irene did not want to explore the wonders of the world with her friends. It was more of a want of her father to try to protect her from the outside world.

"We are going into town tonight," Jo-Ann began to unfold their plans for the evening. "Irene, do you think that your Dad will let you go?"

Irene began to make excuses ahead of time, knowing that her father would have reasons to limit any venture beyond the farm. "You know I have chores to do." Irene did not look up from her task, she continued to slide hands up then down the cow's tits.

"After your chores? We can leave after you have finished all of this farm work," Jo-Ann pleaded, as she leaned over the stall's boarded gate. "Oh, say you will come with us."

Pleading in the same plaintive voice, the girls crowded Jo-Ann on the gate, "Please say yes, please."

No answer came from Irene, while the three girls waited with eyes wide and mouths agape. Irene shrugged shoulders. Placing her head against the cow's inside flank, she began to state reasons why the outing would not happen, "My Dad will not let me go. He has reasons. You know how strict he can be."

"Yes, we know," Sandy spoke for the rest of the girls in her own brash manner. "He would find fault with a Sunday School meeting on a Saturday night, at a church, with ten chaperones, a Nun, a Priest and two holly than thou Bishops."

"See, and you think he is going to let me go into town on a Friday night. He will probably give me a lecture about it, then send me to bed early." Irene slowly rocked her disappointed head into the cow's side.

If only Irene had a older brother, then maybe her father would not be the way he was, maybe he was disappointed that she was a girl and not a first born male.

All felt that it would be worthless to ask Irene's father. Sandy knew that there might be hope if they were to find a fool proof scheme. Talk carried on within the confines of the barn. Only the twitching ears of the livestock listened without condemnation. Efforts were contributed to the plan that would enable the four girls to go into town.

Irene's friend's Families were somewhat liberal with the upbringing of their children. Irene's Mother seemed to want her to experience life. It was her Father that was conservative to the point of denying her simple pleasures. When he spoke, his words were final. New morality, and new ways of society were a damnation in his eyes. Joshua wanted to run his family the way he ran his farm, by the book.

It has been known to mean, in the words of a saying, that behind a great man is a woman just as great. Behind every man, there is a woman that implants thoughts into the mind of her man. Sitting back with a simple smile on their faces, they would let the man think that he had arrived at a conclusion by himself. Do men let women think this way? Do men make decisions in favor of the women, for the simple reason that they love them?

A tall slim man, though years of age showed wrinkles in a face of a man in his early fifties, he stood tall and proud. Josh, as his wife Sarah addressed him, was the head of the family, and made all the important decisions. Sarah, a motherly figure of a woman surely instilled her share of ideas into Josh's mind. Irene's forthcoming situation would require the assistance of Sarah, to Convince Josh to make a right judgement.

Working with thoughts concentrated on the mechanical apparatus of his 49-International tractor, he did not notice Sarah approaching.

"Josh, I need to talk to you."

Josh turned with a start, letting a wrench clank against the tractors manifold. If he was a man of profanity, surely words would have flowed. "Do not come sneaking up behind me like that!" Josh wanted to raise his voice, he decided against it when he caught a glimpse of his wife's tender eyes. "You are liable to give me a heart-attack."

"I do not think so," Sarah's voice was soft with a bit of an edge. "You are too mean and bull-headed. It is possible that you will live to be a hundred and be just as cantankerous."

"I have work to do woman. Is it now that you have to bother me?" Josh picked up the chrome wrench and clanked it against the rusted nut holding down the manifold. "At the moment I am busy." Returning to the work, he tried to avoid any further discussion with Sarah.

"I was talking with Mrs. Carty today, Zoe's mother, Irene's friend." A clanking of a hammer against cast iron interrupted Sarah's words. "Are you listening to me Josh, Joshua?"

"Yes, yes, I see."

Sarah did not seem to be intimidated by anything Josh was doing or saying. Living with a man like Josh showed her how to be patient and easy going, to combat the things that Josh did to bother her. Josh's work continued on the tractor with hammering louder then is normally required. Thinking that Sarah had taken the hint to leave, Josh grinned with a little devilish glow in his eyes.

Suddenly, Josh jumped, letting the hammer drop through the motor area to the ground below. Turning, he faced Sarah, his brown eyes to her green eyes set into a soft complexion. "You are still here?"

"Josh, this may be important." Sarah's eyes pierced deep into Josh, looking behind his brown eyes.

Josh bellowed his words under a breath. If he had let go with full volume, the neighbours a mile away would have heard. "I thought you were gone, do you have things to do, cooking or something?"

"If you do not take time to listen to what I have to say, you may not have a supper to enjoy tonight."

A silence fell over the work area. Sarah and Josh glared at each other, waiting for the other to give-in first. There was a devil in one, and angels floating around the other. Josh knew that there would be no work accomplished until Sarah had her say.

"Okay, I am all ears. Please be brief, I have plenty of work to finish."

"As I was saying, I was talking with Mrs. Carty today. It seems that the girls, Irene's friends, are planning to go into town tonight and they want Irene to go with them."

The words had barely left Sarah's lips when a voice of authority cut into the story being retold. "Out of the question, she is not going into town tonight, or any other night and that is final!"

Sarah continued speaking as if not noticing the rude interruption from her husband. "Our daughter will be turning nineteen in another month. By that time she could be considered an old maid by her friend's standards."

"I do not care. The city is no place for a young girl."

Josh's voice was becoming louder when realizing that his words were losing ground.

"Now, if she wants to meet a nice young man in the city, that just happened to be a farmer's son, and they were to get along well . . .," Sarah thought for a moment while her husband's ears hung onto every word waiting for her to continue. "an extra hand around here would surely be welcomed, instead of having a flock of girls getting under your feet. Honey, do you think so? You would not have to work as hard."

Josh pretended not to be listening. "I can not afford to hire a hired hand."

A smile lit up on Sarah's face, she knew he was coming around to her way of thinking. "Now, if Irene was to find a nice farm boy and they were to get married, soon there would be grand children. Just think how nice it would be to have a son-in-law and grand kids working the farm. There on the porch we would be rocking comfortably in our golden years."

Leaving Josh to contemplate his thoughts, Sarah left saying that she was going to bake some mouth-watering pies for the man in her life.

Repairs to the tractor was attempted. Thoughts of having a helping hand around the farm seemed to have more preference at the moment. Josh knew that he did not want Irene to become an old maid. Falling further into the back of his mind was the other side of the story. What if Irene became entrapped in the virtues of the city, swallowed up by the candy coatings that hid the ugly side of life. He would have to think about it a bit longer. Maybe the situation would go away, then he would not have to deal with it at all.

"I have an idea," Zoe bubbled with excitement. Jumping down form the gate, Zoe smiled as she raised her hands. "We will ask your Pa if you can go . . .," Zoe erased her words with a swipe of her hand. "You stay here, we will butter your father up before you ask him."

"Sure," Sandy excitingly said. "He can not say no to us, we are not his daughters."

New excitement faded from Irene's cream-coloured cheeks. "You do not know my father, nothing will change his mind once he has made it up to say no."

"It is worth a try." Zoe could be just as stubborn at times. "Come on girls, we will get him to say yes."

Irene watched the threesome leave the barn, there was hope in her thoughts, but despair was felt in her heart. Hearing the closing of the barn door brought Irene back to reality, she leaned into the cow, continuing to coax milk from the cow's udder.

With the confidence of seasoned wranglers, the three girls headed towards Irene's Dad. Confidence quickly withered when they were able to see the frown on Mr. Watson's face. A cool chill walked up the spines of the once brave girls. There was no chance of turning back, Mr. Watson had cast protruding eyes upon the approaching starlets. Walking the thirty-feet towards the tractor seemed to take an eternity for the girls. Once they were in front of him, they had wished for more time and distance. Each girl tried not to look Mr. Watson directly in the eyes, even Sandy was not hardened enough to stare him down. Zoe attempted to giggle innocently, it seemed awkward.

"Good afternoon ladies," Mr. Watson's voice was soft and most quiet in tone as he addressed the somewhat perturbed girls.

"Good afternoon," said the girls simultaneously, each confused a bit. This did not seem to be the mannerism usually portrayed by Mr. Watson.

After wiping hands with a rag, a slight smile creased the corner of his mouth. He stood facing three girls standing frozen to fence posts in the dead of winter. Jo-Ann realizing that they were staring at each other without saying anything, prompted her to give an elbow to Zoe's ribs. Usually, Zoe was the spokesperson of the group.

Finding her tongue, Zoe began to spurt out words that confused everyone present. "Irene would like . . ., if you Mr. Watson would . . ., I mean we, she would be with us . . ., she, Irene would ask, but we are . . ., asking now."

Jo-Ann and Sandy tried to help Zoe explain the situation. Three voices were all chattering something different to a man, like all other men, are only able to listen to one voice and only one explanation. Mr. Watson tried to sort out the gibbering, the more he listened the wider his mouth stretched open.

"Hold it girls." Holding his index finger to lips, Mr. Watson asked for silence. "Sh . . ., Sh. Let me see if I can figure out what you are trying to say."

A threesome of girls reluctantly became quiet, each clinging to every word spoken by Irene's father. A man that was once described as a tyrant, seemed to be shed of the noted moniker. An awe fell over the girls. This was not the Mr. Watson they all knew. Maybe there was a heart in the man, the girls had hope.

"Tell me if I am wrong? I think the three of you have something planned, and you would like Irene to join in on your escapades." Mr. Watson gave a broad grin as he looked towards the sky. The girls understood it to be an impression of a man deep in thought. "It is surprising how fast the years have come and gone. How fast you girls have grown up. Soon you will be raising a family of your own."

Faces became slightly red with an innocent embarrassment, they were surely caught of guard. Coloured eyes exchanged bewildered thoughts, thoughts and feelings that were mutual. They never expected that Irene's father would ever talk about things of that sort, especially to them.

"I think it is time that you girls, young ladies, should get out and meet some fine young men," rambled on Mr. Watson, his hand itched at a day-old growth of beard. Lowering eyes from the sky, he added, "Maybe the four of you should go into town to see a movie. I will tell you what, I will even drive you there then pick you all up after you have had a night on the town." Mr. Watson's eyes focused on the girls, while anticipating an agreeable reply.

Zoe quickly accepted Mr. Watson's proposal. At the same time she changed the transportation situation. "That is a great idea, Mr. Watson. It would be nice of you to drive us into town around seven O'clock. Oh . . ., my brother, Phil, wants to pick us up later to take us home, you will not be inconvenienced or obliged to fetch us, thank you for the offer."

Zoe smiled broadly with a grin prompting the other girls to join in with assorted smiles. With fast talk, she had left Mr. Watson confounded about the latter conversation. A grinning smile that once lit up Mr. Watson's face, faded. Left standing there was the face of a man, as a boy that had lost a favorite toy. Zoe and the two girls turned to leave.

"Thank you Mr. Watson." Zoe smiled back towards the man standing alone beside a disabled tractor. "See you latter," said Zoe from the open gate leading to the field.

Holding back giggles and laughter, the girls ran enthusiastically back towards the barn, each wanting to tell the great news to Irene. Barnyard sounds between the house, where Mrs. Watson Stood sweeping the porch and where Mr. Watson stood near the tractor, where overcome with the sounds of happiness being celebrated by the girls.

Zoe began relating the conversation they had with Irene's father, "You can go, he said you can go!"

"Yeah, your Dad even said that he would drive us into town," said Jo-Ann to a surprised Irene. "He gave the impression that it was his idea that you should go into town with us."

"Un . . ., hu," Sandy said between sentences. "He said, we should go and meet some nice young men."

"I do not believe you. My father would never say something like that." Irene brushed back hair from her face with the back side of a hand. Her eyes seemed moist with happiness or disappointment. "I think he would rather see me become an old maid."

"Honest!" Three voices simultaneously said.

With sincerity, Zoe attempted to convince Irene, "If you do not believe us, and you do not go with us, you will become an old maid. Do you want your father to be happy or do you want to be happy?"

"We are going into town, the four of us and your father is driving us." informed Sandy, her hands placed on hips with a gesture of authority. "At seven sharp, you had better be ready. We will be back expecting your father to drive us. Irene Watson you had better be dressed to tantalize the young men your father expects us to meet."

Surely the girls were serious, but to Irene's way of reasoning, she did not believe them, though she wanted to. Irene did not know how to react, so kept everything in a friendly perspective. "That will be nice. Seven O'clock it is."

Smiles returned to the girls' faces, with hints of childish disobedience in their eyes. If only fathers were able to see into the minds of their daughters. What were the girls willing to do, what were they getting Irene into?

"We have to go now and get ready for tonight," implied an anxious Jo-Ann. "Let's go girls."

Behind the swinging barn door the departing girls left Irene alone to continue milking the cows. Several chickens and un-milked cows gathered to listen to her verbal thoughts. Had her father said what was allegedly said? Would her friends play games with her emotions? Being able to go out with friends meant too much to emotions to be played with. Irene knew it would be best to talk to her mother first, before her father said something to her.

Through the motions of the day, Irene finished chore after chore with her mind somewhere in the clouds. By design, she avoided any confrontation with her parents. When Mrs. Watson called out super time, it was time for the family to gather. There was no way to avoid this assembly.

Conversations from the younger members of the family were of no importance. Each of the three elder members of the family waited patiently, waiting for the other to bring up the subject of importance. Mrs. Watson's wondrous meal was near completion before the first words on the subject were spoken.

Mrs. Watson passed a piece of bread to a youngest daughter. "Josh," with a demanding eye she glared at her husband. "do you have something to say?"

Trying to preserve time, Mr. Watson answered slowly, "Say, say something about what?"

"Do you want to spend the night with Duke, in the dog house, my love?"

A small cluster of giggles came from the young daughters, as their attention was drawn to their Mom and Dad. Father cast a look of punishment upon them, a scornful look that sent chills down their spines. Only the youngest child continued to giggle, her fathers looks did not deter her enjoyment.

Sitting back in the chair, a bit more relaxed, he took a napkin to wipe the mood from his face. "I had the pleasure Irene, to talk with some of your friends today. Nice young girls from good families. I know their fathers from way back when. Went to school with them way back when."

Soft giggles came from the young daughters. Mrs. Watson raised a cautious eyebrow to the girls then gained her husband's main train of thought.

"Well that is not important. As I was saying to your friends, Irene, I said you all are becoming young ladies and soon will be getting married and leaving home." He nodded his head along with the mocking from young daughters. "Then I suggested that all four of you should go into town, to a show or something, maybe meet some nice young men. They agreed that I had a great idea." With assurance, Mr. Watson leaned forward and rested elbows on the table edge. "I think . . .,"

"Daddy, Daddy," said the youngest daughter, knowing about table manners and that they were to be abided by, and by everyone.

"That you . . .,"

"Daddy, Daddy."

"What do you want?" said with a temper rising, Mr. Watson tried to control it while smiling down upon a blue-eyed daughter. "Yes dear, what is it, speak up?"

"You have your elbows on the table. You always tell us not to put our elbows on the table. That is a no no!" A small smile was cast up towards her Pa.

Slowly, the elbows were removed while Josh tried to collect composure. "That is right dear. Thank you for reminding me." Turning back to his wife and Irene, he tried to continue where he had left off, "Yes, where was I, I was saying, ah . . .,"

"You were saying something about going into town tonight dear," Mrs. Watson said without making the obvious too obvious.

"Yes, maybe you should join them. I offered to drive all of you there and back, but they said a brother would drive everyone home."

Irene sat with an open mouth, unable to comprehend what had just been said. Her mother was a bit set back, she had expected to hear a lecture on the virtues of good clean living versus the sinfulness of city life. Then again, he could be waiting for a more appropriate moment.

Beginning to talk, Mr. Watson pulled a pocket watch from his coveralls. Noting the time, he motioned to Irene. "It is getting late, your friends will be here soon. Go and get ready."

There was plenty of time, yet avoiding any change of mind, Irene excused herself from the table. In the inside corner of her right eye a bead of emotion lingered. Her father fidgeted with the place settings on the table. Mrs. Watson smiled with satisfaction as she began to clear the table. She was pleased that the seed she had planted in her husband's mind had matured.

Thoughts of lecturing Irene about the perils of the big city had entered Josh's mind, but it became difficult to say anything in a crowed car. The gaiety of the girls interrupted his every word, their constant chatter prevented him from communicating any thought. Mr. Watson's newly acquired smile diminished to the norm of his previously described character. He felt sorry for the fathers of these girls. Maybe their fathers hoped they would meet a boy and hurriedly move away from home.

"Thanks for the ride Mr. Watson," swiftly said Zoe, who waved to the girls to get out of the car as fast as possible. "Thank you, bye."

Irene shying looked back towards her father. "Thank you, Dad."

Josh attempted a slight smile as he looked for the first time at his grown daughter. In his eyes she was very pretty, though the flowered dress seemed a contrast to the hip attire of her friends.

Irene watched the tail lights of her father's car blend into the hundreds of other flashing tail lights. It was as if her father was abandoning her for the first time in her lifetime. Stepping back onto the sidewalk, Irene joined the giddiness of friends.

"Let's go to some fancy hotel, a disco place."

"No Jo-Ann, some real wild place where we can live dangerously." A blissful smile big enough to light up the sky prevailed over most of Zoe's face.

Sandy was curious to see if Irene was still under the influence of her father. "Where would you like to go Irene?"

"I do not know, maybe a movie show." An awkwardness surfaced on her face as she spoke. "I never really thought about a destination."

Bringing the attention back to herself, Zoe wanted a decision. "Make up your mind girls. We are single and free, and out to be naughty."

Boo viewed the young lady with respectful glances, he did not want to be too forward. "Most friends address me by the name of Boo. I do not intend to frighten as the name may imply."

Irene held onto Boo's arm as a scared child would, she walked beside him with an arm under and over his in an old-fashioned embrace. Hints of blush showed on her cheeks. She was able to sense her movements, and his. In the warm breeze, her dress flowed and curly hair bounced, his western style boots made a silent crunch with each step.

Breaking the girl's silence, Boo brought her back to the present by asking, "I take it, you have a name to suit your elegance."

Looking modestly upward at Boo's six-foot height, Irene awoke from a dream, she answered, "Yes, ah, my name is Irene."

"A lyrical impression of a girl to be immortalized in a song. I hope I do not have to say 'Goodnight Irene' too early." Boo watched a smile build across her face. "Tell me the names of your followers." Boo peeked over a shoulder to see if Irene's three friends were tagging along.

For some reason the once happy threesome had a despairing glare on their faces. In muffled voices they talked between themselves only to give a half hearted smile when Irene introduced them to Boo.

"My best friends, Zoe, Sandy and Jo-Ann."

"Ladies," acknowledged Boo. "I shall be your navigator through the night life of this city. Your protector if need be." Boo gave an honest smile with as much friendliness as needed to be accepted by the girls.

"We would like to visit all the night spots in town, dance, meet guys and dance the night away," demanded Sandy, showing a domineering attitude.

"Then let's go. This way if you please." With Irene in arm, Boo lead the way into the first bar along the strip of illusions.

After several drinks and dances, the girls began to warm up and accept Boo. Bar after bar, sometimes going back and forth to visit a previous bar just for the fun, the three dateless girls added and discarded partners at will.

At first, Boo's intentions were focused on seeking a body for the evening. There was something about Irene that intrigued Boo, a sense of honesty, of untouched purity. Both sipped soft drinks. Seldom danced. Talk occupied their minds, drawing both deeper into the other's morale integrity. Boo knew better then to assume anything but respect and courtesy, yet there was an attraction that both felt towards the other. Irene knew that Nights on white steeds did not just ride into one's life. Anyone of the other girls would have welcomed Boo into their beds. Maybe it was what he could not have from Irene that attracted him to her.

Hours passed like seconds of a minute hand spinning freely beneath a glass slipper. Soon the girls would be leaving, entering back into their daily lives. When the time of departure arrived, Boo would be left behind, left to seek shelter and sleep. Boo held the tips of Irene's fingers softly caressing a milk soft texture.

"We have to go," announced Jo-Ann after downing the remaining liquor in her glass. "It is two-thirty, my brother will be waiting for us."

Irene's eyes caught Boo's, they seemed to say that time had passed too quickly, this Cinderella story was almost over. Words now seemed to be at a loss. Irene seemed to have words forming on lips that did not take shape. Somehow, Boo was letting a feeling, a wanting, slip through finger.

Lightly grasping Boo's hand, Irene followed the other girls out onto the sidewalk, towards the waiting car of Jo-Ann's brother. With the excitement of the night and the influences of alcohol, the girls carried the party atmosphere with them. Into Phil's car they piled, no-one questioned Boo, as he slipped into the seat beside Irene. Holding onto each other's hand there was no need of talk. Neither Boo nor Irene knew what was in-store for them, as if they were flowing along in life on a happy breeze.

When a body say's it is time to stop the party, the body becomes quiet and heads slowly tilt to a soft resting spot. One by one the girls nodded off into slumber. Irene rested a happy face against Boo's shoulder. Phil, minding his own business, felt no need to meddle. Only once did Boo and Phil exchange a pleasant hello.

One after another the girls were dropped off at the ends of long driveways. With feeble voices, they offered a goodnight then dragged feet along gravel driveways towards the comfort of welcoming beds. Zoe, Sandy then Irene. Coming to a stop at the end of the Watson's driveway, Phil waited for Irene and her friend to depart. Groaning a goodbye, Jo-Ann did not bother to open eyes. Boo closed the car door and watched Phil's Camaro blend into the prairie night.

A single porch light, flickering through marauding moths, beckoned Irene home. Boo kissed soft lips that did not pull away. A gentle kiss, a non assuming kiss. Irene backed away with a puzzled look. Something was wrong, had she let her fantasy dream linger for too long.

"Boo, you can not stay here." With shacking hands, she pressed against Boo's chest. "How are you going to get back to town?"

"I have no way of getting back to town." Boo pulled a small ribbon from Irene's hair that let curls cascade down onto the back of her neck. "I am not from this Province, I have no idea where to go." Boo leaned and kissed a soft cheek with several light touches. Boo's voice whispered, "Where would you like me to go?"

Irene's thoughts were not coherent at the present time. Racing through her mind were visions of moonlit starry nights and thoughts of her father's lectures.

"It would be nice to stay with you."

"No, No!" Irene hurriedly said, realizing what Boo had whispered into her ear. "My father would never permit such a thing. If he even found you sleeping in the barn, I dread the thought of what he might do."

An air of aggressiveness prevailed over Boo, he reached for Irene, drawing her closer to his warm body. "I am not afraid to be here with you."

Irene's intentions were to dismiss Boo from the premises. Boo's romantic advances became more and more accepted. Hands caressed her sides then pressed her body closer to his. The warmth of bodies together encouraged the essence of reluctant ecstasy. Boo's hand roamed upward to the firmness of Irene's breasts, he could feel the nipple rising beneath the silken bra.

Trembling, Irene pushed away unwillingly saying as she turned away. "I have never . . ., right now I can not."

Delicate blonde hair shone in the moonlight. A figure of an emotional girl ran towards the comfort of home and family. Left standing like a fool, Boo questioned his intentions and present circumstances. Town was too far away. Irene warned him about sleeping in the barn. Boo watched Irene's dress float away down the driveway. Looking around into the darkness, Boo pondered the thought of standing in a current spot for the rest of the night.

"Where are you going, Josh?" Mrs. Watson whispered as she reached out trying to grab his night shirt.

Josh grunted. "I am going to have a talk with our daughter. Do you realize what time it is?"

Reaching around the floor with feet he searched for misplaced slippers. Sarah attempted to restrain him from doing anything drastic.

"No, you are not, you old fool. Let her enjoy her memories, without you spoiling them by an unwanted interrogation," Sarah's voice was stern with a tone meant to be abided by.

In mid motion, Josh stopped with reluctance in putting on the other half of a house-coat. Both became silent when the creaking of Irene's bedroom door closed. Mr. Watson's temper calmed, knowing that his daughter was now safely home. Leaning back onto the pillow, Sarah smiled with motherly content. On the edge of the bed, Josh sat for a few moments before rolling under the covers. A silence wove throw the century farm house, except in Irene's room.

From her darkened room, Irene peered through a window, tears reflected in the glass from a pale moon-light. It was not a cry, or a sniffle, rather a confusion of feelings that seemed new to her. Irene gazed through wet eyes out over the farm fields. From her room, she could not see the driveway, she wondered if Boo was still standing there at the end. What was he doing, was he now heading back into town and out of her life. Moments passed, Irene hugged a soft rag doll and lay curled upon the bed.

On the spot, Boo decided that he was not making the long walk back into town. Silently and inquisitively, he looked around the farm until an object of interest became visible. A ladder of sufficient length lay propped against a fence. Carrying the ladder across the front yard was of no importance in the lateness of the night, there was a more prevalent thought in mind.

Silhouetted against the wall like a thief in the night, Boo leaned the ladder against the house wall. A rustling of a shrub silenced the night crickets. By chance, Boo had hoped that the window above was that of Irene's. A light tap thudded as the ladder rested against the window sill. With each step on the aging rungs, a creaking sound was sure to be heard by cows in the distant field.

Boo pressed his face to the cool glass pane. A deformed mug of a face peered into the darkness of the room. Boo would have to take a chance. With an index finger he began to tap against the glass. Tap, tap, tap, rhythm of a Morris-code repeated through the air waves. Boo desperately hoped that this was Irene's room. Again, the tap, tap, tap sounded.

Irene pressed a hand to her nose to stop a sniffle, when assuming she had heard a taping sound. Again, her ears had picked up the odd sound. Stepping from the bed, her long flannel night gown reached to brush the floor. Sneaking towards the window, she squinted past the curtains. At the suddenness of seeing each other they recoiled in opposite directions.

Boo grabbed for a tighter grip as he felt himself leaning too far backwards. A gasp came to a silent mouth of Irene, she hesitated then reached to raise the window casing. Soft strong hands griped at Boo's arms drawing him into the room. Laying halfway into the room, Boo relaxed his body with relief of knowing that the hard ground was no-longer a destination. Panting, Irene griped Boo's belt, forcing his body the rest of the way into the room. Seeing Boo sprawled on the floor, Irene covered her mouth with shaking hands. Her body shivered as if caught in the depths of a winter's chill.

Rolling to his side, Boo swallowed the beauty of the person standing before him. Even under the rays of the moon, her face glowed with a glitter of wetness on cheeks. Boo exhaled with delight and relief.

"Thank you," sounded Boo's first words. "I could have fallen and hurt myself."

Irene's voice trembled, "What are you doing here?" Her voice became stern in a matter-of-facts. "Hurt . . .! If my father finds you in here, in my room, he will probably shoot you. You then will be under ground for eternity." Irene knelt on the floor in front of Boo.

Boo reached out to fondle and brush from her face curls of limp hair. "You would not scream for his presence, would you," Boo said as he knelt in front of her. "I have no place to go, no place to rest my tired bones." Looking straight into confused eyes, Boo milked the situation. "I would not be able to cope with the coolness of the night, the wild animals, the potential danger of a city boy lost in the wilderness." Boo's sincerity was now off track. Would Irene see through it, or see what was really Boo's intentions. "You would not want something to happen to me, would you?"

Deep green eyes of innocence were being swallowed by Boo's shit brown eyes which were as full as the bull he was feeding her. Whether right or wrong, a conflict was waging war in Irene's mind. Boo leaned closer, kissing her tenderly on lips that ached for experience. A kiss to preoccupy her thoughts.

There was a shyness, an innocence of a young woman untouched which showed in Irene's eyes. Within those eyes was also the curiosities of testing life's wonders that she wanted to indulge in. With caution, Irene slipped arms around Boo's neck, teasing his long-ish brown hair.

Drawing closer, their bodies sought the warmth of a woven rug covering a hard wood floor. When morning found them enwrapped in each other's arms would Irene request Boo to leave. For the moment their thoughts embraced each other. The intensities of the moment over-shadowed the details of the future.

Kicking off boots onto the floor, Boo drew Irene's soft flannel night gown upward. Hearing the clump of heavy boots, Irene backed away climbing to the comfort of the bed. Taking a slight breath, Boo moved towards the bed pressing her body against the beading. Unfamiliar to the procedures, Irene fumbled with Boo's shirt buttons. Under the flannel gown hands caressed long firm legs.

Anticipating a quickness of undone buttons that slowed, Boo stood with legs straddling Irene. Watchful eyes undressed Boo, as he removed a shirt then unclasped a belt buckle letting jeans fall. Irene wished for the experiences that she often noticed the farm animals exchange. In the semi darkness, her eyes ventured over Boo's body. Boo eased himself down against her quivering body.

Raising up the flannel gown, naked skin touched naked skin. Firm breasts rose, she felt a rising sensation against a leg. Wonderment of love making that Irene anticipated happening in her life was now occurring with a blurriness of thoughts. A body untouched quivered, lips parted as tongues touched. Raising knees, Irene squeezed hands across Boo's shoulders. In the stillness of the room, only the slight movement of the bed set the wooden frame to squeak against metal rails.

In advancing years, Josh had noticed that his ability to sleep through the night without the need to urinate had become less and less. Easing from the bed, he stepped into slippers to make the journey down the hallway to the bathroom. In a state of slumber, Josh knew the way to the bathroom, but there was a foreign sound that pulsated into eardrums. Stopping at Irene's door, he listened to the sound that he was far too familiar with. After knowing the pleasure of participating in the creation of daughters, he knew what was taking place in his daughter's room.

On tip toes, Josh hastened back to the hall closet to retrieve a shotgun. Fumbling with a hurried motion, he rummaged over boxes and kids toys to the hidden door that housed the shotgun. At this point in time, his temper was beyond the point of caring about the quietness of actions.

Reaching the threshold of what both Boo and Irene were venturing towards, suddenly could not be savored. Heavy footsteps sent the floor boards creaking in the hallway.

"My father," Irene said, swallowing a breath. "Go . . ., hide in the closet."

Gathering discarded clothing, Boo scrambled to the security of the room's closet. Among the aroma of woman's clothing and the cramp confines of the closet, Boo attempted to dress. Irene grabbed a hair brush and began to comb through locks, as she sat on the edge of the bed.

Bursting into the room without knocking, Mr. Watson flicked on the bedroom light. Both Irene and father squinted under the harshness of the light.

"Dad!" a startled Irene said. "What is the matter? Why do you have your shotgun?"

Mr. Watson did not answer, his eyes scanned the room, every inch of the room. There was something amiss in this room, under his roof. With the barrel of the shotgun, he lifted the corner of the bed sheet and then bent over to peek under it. Turning quickly he looked behind the opened door when his eye caught the look of leather of a man's boot by the window.

In the confines of the closet, Boo listened to the footsteps of a man pace about the room. Though winded from the pleasure of their encounter, Boo hesitated to take a deep breath.

Josh stepped closer to the boot. An extended shotgun barrel lifted the boot to a standing position. Josh turned to face his daughter, there was a disappointed profile on his lips.

"All the girls are starting to wear boots of that style," Irene grasped at the first thoughts that entered her mind. "My friends are all wearing them."

Irene looked directly into her father's eyes burning fiery red. There was nothing that he wanted to say to his daughter. Standing, facing the closet door, he cocked back the hammers of the double barrel shotgun. Like a scene from a western movie, the disgruntled father aimed the weapon from hip height towards the closet door.

Standing half dressed, Boo did not move, his eyes peering at the inside of the door. Without seeing through the wooden panel, it was as if Boo knew what was happening on the other side. Boo heard the twisting of the door handle then the piercing of light hit his eyes. A hammer head struck without an explosion. Boo opened one eye to see the second hammer striking the firing pin. A chill rippled down his spine. Memories of a life time flashed before his eyes. Boo remembered the words of Salami's Mother, he recalled her saying 'make sure you have clean underwear on in case you . . . .'

"Dammit, dammit, that woman!" Josh stomped a foot and broke open the shotgun.

Irene lowered hands from a tear covered face. Inside of her body she could feel her heart shaking from what might have happened if the shotgun had exploded.

Opening an eye to the success of a misfired shotgun, a smile came to Boo's lips. In his utopia of the situation, Boo searched thoughts for something to say, an introduction of sorts. "Howdy," was all that came to Boo's lips.

"You are dam lucky you are not leaking blood all over the floor," Josh replied with anger. "Sarah!" he yelled with a voice of a jagged knife cutting through the silence of his house and home.

Clad in a housecoat, Sarah cut a fine figure of a woman, Irene twenty years from now. Without tying the front of her housecoat, that revealed an ample bosom beneath a silken night gown, she went to sit beside Irene.

"Sarah, tie up your housecoat and look decent." Josh blocked the view between Boo and the women sitting on the bed. "Tie up your front, this, he does not need to see, he has, confound-it Sarah, I told you not to hide my shotgun shells." Josh pocked the barrel towards Boo's middle. "For a situation exactly like this, is what I need to have shells loaded in my shotgun."

Sarah seemed not to be upset at the sight of a male intruder in the house. Looking at her daughter, and the type of tears and emotion being presented, Sarah knew that the stranger was invited. "Josh, your are upsetting Irene. Put that gun down, you are making that young man nervous."

Boo returned her gesture with a polite smile. Being half undressed, Boo awkwardly fumbled with hands and clothes. A man with a loud demeaning voice and a shotgun poking at his middle, Boo knew who was boss. Pulling up pants and stuffing loose shit tails into them, Boo tried to look decent under the circumstances.

Sarah kissed and pampered her daughter as Josh kicked the lone boot over to the intruder. Back and forth, Josh swung the shotgun towards the open door. "Out the door you go, and down the stairs. No sudden moves."

Bending down to pull the boot on, Boo hopped towards the exit, away from the presence of Irene, whom he seemed to care for. Unlike the women that he had met and forgotten about back in Steeltown, or the ones he had met so far on this trip, Irene was different. Boo felt altered, fresh, a new person around her. At the bottom of the stairs, Boo searched for a comfortable position to stand and place hands.

Boo knew Irene's father meant business when several shotgun shells were retrieved from the drawer of the telephone stand. Suddenly, he looked twice as big and meaner then a bull guarding its herd. Being in the custody of the police would be better than being before a man that was placing twelve gauge slugs into a shotgun.

"Take one sudden move and we will have a hard time picking you off of the floor." Josh pointed the weapon towards Boo's chest. Holding it with one hand, he used the other to dial a telephone number.

The cops, Boo really did not want. It was enough to have the O.P.P. in Ontario looking for him. Running was a cowardly thing to do. Boo was not cowardly, he just did not want to get shot at. Waiting there in the sitting room of the beautiful old home, Boo listened to the telephone conversation.

"Hello Jock, Jock this is Josh, wake up." No answer was returned over the line. Josh waited for a slight response from his brother before continuing. "Jock you have fifteen minutes to get over here, do not interrupt, I will explain later. Bring your shotgun and on your way over pick up the Reverend Walls." Josh paused while the party at the other end talked. "Yeah, the Reverend. Do not ask questions now."

It was obvious that Boo had questions, but, when he tried to voice them, he stared down the barrel of shinny black shotgun. Further inquiry at this time would be needless. Boo had no need for alterations to his breathing appendage.

"Fifteen minutes, and do not show up without the preacher." Josh returned the receiver to its saddle with a forced slam. Glaring with contempt, Josh spoke. "Sit awhile, we have a long morning ahead of us."

Cautiously sitting down as told, Boo prepared himself for the worst of the worst. Two and two was not hard to add up. There was to be a shotgun wedding with Boo as the invited groom. Then again it could be two minus one with the preacher saying a few words over a reclining body.

Dawn came with the early morning light lighting up the beauty of well oiled wood walls and furniture left by ancestors. With the light came the kinfolk by word of mouth. Upwards of twenty strangers popped their heads into the sitting room to gawk at the prize specimen that Josh had trapped. Boo seemed indifferent to the gathering, his thoughts were of Irene and what he had put her through. If only he could have escaped with her before he let his lower anatomy do his thinking. Only a head seeking pleasure would get a man into this type of trouble.

Through the open door leading into the kitchen, Boo listened to the voices discussing the situation. Irene's father, the preacher, other men and old ladies giving their piece of mind for all that it was worth. One voice echoed the same words whenever there was a lull in the conversation. "Let's put him out of his misery."

Boo eyed his surroundings, searching for a way to escape. Small framed-in windows on one side of the room would not let a pigeon through. Up the fireplace chimney, no, he was not Santa Claus. Out through the sliding doors right into a lanky kid with spiked hair shouldering a rifle, not likely.

"He has to do right by this family," Irene's father, still in a night shirt, began to raise his voice at the preacher. "Do you know what he has done to my daughter. He has shamed her."

An eloquent soft voice of the preacher responded, "Josh, you must not subject your loving daughter and this young man to a life of marriage without their consent." With an ironed white hanky, the preacher dabbed at the hairline of a toupee. "In the eyes of our almighty savior, He would favor these two children of God to be in love with each other." Sweat formed on the preacher's forehead, again, he dabbed with a linen hanky. "Our Lord will forgive sinners."

"Put him out of his misery," repeated the irritating voice as he added. "Shoot the scoundrel."

Some kin cheered at the suggestion, while the preacher politely scowled and dabbed at his forehead. Josh waved the shotgun in the air, demanding silence.

"We are not going to shoot, hell, I do not even know what to call him. We will not shoot him, not right this minute anyway." Josh shook his head while he thought out loud. "I need a hand on this farm and he is going to earn his keep working it, even if I have to be at his back with a shotgun twenty-four hours a day."

Silence came to the household. Boo strained to hear their whispers, but every sudden move he made invoked the strange kid outside to twitch. Just as sudden when the voices stopped, they increased with gusto and volume. Boo stiffened as the sliding doors opened and people poured into the room. From the kitchen, the rest of the kin entered the den of damnation.

Frozen in the seat, Boo felt countless eyes peering at him from all directions. Eyes of anger, curiosity and wonderment explored Boo's entire body. Boo felt like an actor standing naked on a stage for all to see, with no place to hide. If only to be able to draw the stage curtain.

In the background, the sobs of Irene were faintly heard below the gibber-jabber of the assembled group. Boo wanted to reach out to her, to hide behind her, to be protected from her kin. Sarah stood by Iren's side, with the same emotions her daughter was feeling, but she found it hard to speak among in-laws.

Josh stepped forward with the shotgun resting over an arm. The barrels were still pointing in Boo's direction. "You have exactly ten minutes to propose to my daughter," His voice sent chills up and down Boo's spine. Josh raised his voice, "And the proposal had better be a proposal of marriage."

As if the parting of the waters of biblical times had occurred, the gathered people made room for Boo to see Irene. Boo stared at Irene dressed in a flannel nightgown with a loose shawl draped over shoulders. In front of the sliding doors she stood, alone, being highlighted by the morning sun. From his sitting position, Boo was able to see the silhouette of slender legs beneath Irene's gown. For a moment the thought of an earlier passion had clicked the urge to continue their bonding.

Josh's voice broke Boo's insane thought, "We will be in the next room, and someone will be outside of the house." With agitated hands, Josh motioned for everyone to vacate the room. "Buck, watch the window," spoke Josh to the spike haired kid grinning with anticipated enjoyment. "Ten minutes, that is all," were the last words Irene's father spoke before closing the doors leading to the kitchen.

Boo gestured with hands, shoulders and facial expressions as if he were speaking words of intense meanings. Nothing of importance, or comfort for Irene, vocalized from his moving lips. Irene stood there in innocent beauty. Tears stained her pink cheeks, hands griped the night gown around full hips. Boo wanted to stand and embrace her with strong understanding arms, but how could he. Right now, Boo was as confused as she was. When this night had started, Boo was looking for a one night stand. In and out then leave, but there was a catch distorting his plans, he felt . . . .

Irene broke the silence, speaking through tears and soft sniffles, "For the first time, for my first-time last night, I thought sex would be as wonderful as it was. I had expected to be married first. I wanted last night to happen and was pleased to have it happen."

Irene wiped the wetness of her nose in a hand. Boo probed pockets for a hanky, but was unable to be a gentleman and offer one to her. With a heave, her chest rose as she took in a deep breath.

"I did not expect such a loving moment to turn into such a fiasco. Inside I feel terrible, empty, as if a part of what I love has died."

"It may be me that dies." Boo pointed to the kitchen doors and the spooky kid outside, standing sentry. "Your family are toting enough weapons to get rid of fifty guys like me." Boo paused, thinking of his attitude. "I am sorry that I am the guy that put you into this outlandish situation."

Irene turned away as Boo stood and reached a passionate hand towards her face. With a soft touch, he lifted her face to gaze into deep green eyes of a lush and vibrant meadow. Those eyes melted Boo's heart.

"Do you want what your father demands?" asked Boo, of Irene who slowly rocked her head from side to side. "If I escape, alive, this will all be over for me. Irene, you will still be here, left to live with the scorn from family and by your father."

In Irene's eyes was something new, Boo sensed it, a newfound strength. "I am glad that this has happened. This has given me the strength to decide my own future. As of now I have decided to follow my own rules." Tears stopped flowing. Irene clenched teeth then forced herself to stand tall. "As soon as you can get out of here, the sooner I will be able to get on with my own life."

Irene placed both hands to the sides of Boo's head drawing him to her. A hard forceful kiss of determination, Irene planted on Boo's lips. Boo nodded with a pleased grin.

"At the first chance you have Boo, run for it. While they are chasing you, I will be heading in the opposite direction."

A kinked frown showed on Boo's forehead. "And your kinfolk will be chasing me with loaded buck-shot."

Taking Boo's hand into hers, Irene softly kiss his fingers. "I would like to meet sometime in the future."

A tender moment was lost when the kitchen doors slid open and a mass of people poured in. "Back off boy, you are not married yet," said Josh, sticking the shogun barrel between Boo and Irene. "Is everything settled?" blood shot eyes questioned both victims.

Irene quickly answered, "Yes, everything is settled. We know what is best at this time."

Josh lifted his head over the crowd. "Okay, everyone get ready, preacher. We will have the ceremony on the front lawn. Buck, keep an eye on him."

People began to mill about in different directions. Suddenly the sitting room was left to Boo and Buck, who held a rifle pointed towards Boo's feet. Boo declined looking into the face of a kid with an itchy trigger finger.

"I bet you would rather be cutting heads off of chickens, is that right?" asked Boo, grinning sadistically.

If Boo moved, the kid moved, if Boo needed to take a leak, the kid would be right there. Boo was trapped, there was no escape. If he escaped to the fields and the distant brush, they would track him down. It was their knowledge of the land that prevailed like the familiarity of their own back of the hand. Boo stared out through the sliding glass doors towards the main road a quarter of a mile down the farm's driveway. With a good head start, he could make it, but then where would he go. Traffic on the road seemed scarce and these folks had transportation.

"Where the hell are you, Salami?"

"What did you call me," questioned the startled Kid.

Boo regrouped thoughts. "I was wondering if you all serve salami at shotgun weddings."

To Boo's surprise, Buck talked right up, "At cousin Flo's wedding, I ate a big salami all by myself," he said with a slurred speech.

Now would be the only time Boo had to acquire information, if the kid was obliging. "Do you mind if I ask you a question or two?" The kid nodded yes to Boo's question. "If you, I am only asking, if you were to get married, where would you go for your honey moon?"

"I ain't going to get married."

"No, oh!"

"I am going to travel, maybe up to Calgary to the big rodeo. I like to go on the bus. My Mom took me on the Greyhound bus all the way to Winnipeg." Buck gave a broad smile when he remembered the fun of his past trip.

"You had fun?"

"Yup, me and my Mom."

Boo had hoped he was onto something, maybe this kid would provide a clue to escaping in one piece. "All the way into Winnipeg, on a Greyhound bus. I wish I could take Irene on a Greyhound bus for our honeymoon. Do you think that is a good idea?" Boo felt that maybe he was pushing the matter too far.

"She would, that would be fun, I know, I know, the Greyhound bus drives by, right in front, on the road, right in front." Buck was becoming excited, as if it was his honeymoon he was going on. "You, you and Irene gonna get a ride on the Greyhound bus?"

"When, Bucky boy. When does it go by, we do not want to miss it." Boo leaned out to the edge of the sofa, withholding excitement.

Twisting a wrist, Buck pointed to his watch with a finger. "When this hand gets to this place on the watch."

Bending out to see, Boo looked at the Micky Mouse watch which showed the time to be nine-o-five. Buck was pointing at nine-forty-five. "It comes by in three quarters of an hour?"

Buck bowed his head up and down several times. "Yeah, pretty soon. I watch it go by every day. I am going to go on the Greyhound bus to the Calgary Stampede."

Behind Boo, the kitchen doors sprung open startling him. Josh stuck in his head. "Irene told me your name, and I do not like it." Josh adjusted his Sunday best clothes, then lowered his voice to a civil volume. "Buck, the preacher say's it would be proper to leave all the firearms in the house. Okay Mr. Boo, it is time for the ceremony."

Josh opened the front door leading onto the covered porch where several rocking chairs lined the outside wall. Stepping out onto the weathered boards, Boo looked down on the gathered reception. It was like a last walk to the gallows. People parted, making a path for Boo to walk towards the waiting preacher.

"Son," said the preacher gesturing with an upturned hand to his left. "Stand here my son."

For what seemed like an eternity in hell, Boo stood there with a congregation of future in-laws. Laying behind the preacher, a huge black hairy dog watched Boo shuffle and tap feet that were itching to run. To the distant road, Boo's eyes drifted, hoping not to see a Greyhound bus passing by early. Buck nudged Boo, then pointed to a table filled with food. After a night without food, Boo fought the urge to stay for the meal.

A group sigh interrupted the chatter when they noticed Irene stepping out onto the porch. Sarah fluffed her own wedding gown that accentuated a beautiful young daughter. Boo stopped shuffling and stared with interest. If only under different circumstances, a different time in Boo and Irene's life, maybe this romance would have come true. A wishful fairy tale.

Irene looked directly into Boo's eyes. With the strength she had told Boo she had, she smiled with a glow that lit up his emotions. With a small wink for Boo, Irene collapsed to the porch with the talent of a film legend. Everyone rushed to the steps of the porch. Sarah rested Irene's head in her lap, Josh patted her hand with light taps. Boo turned towards the road only to see the eyes of the black dog staring at him from its resting spot.

In his spot of importance, the preacher looked at Boo with understanding. "Run son. This is the time to head for the hills."

That was all the encouragement Boo needed. At the fastest possible run that he was able to muster, Boo headed down the driveway towards the main road. Suddenly there was a strange feeling, as if the devil himself was breathing down his neck. Boo turned to see some of the men beginning to give chase. Close on his heals was a great giant of a dog with saliva drooling from fangs of hardened spikes.

"Shit, dog, not you too. What is your stake in this matter?" Boo poured more power into tensing legs. "What do I look like, a piece of steak?!"

If in silent-film mode, Boo would have been Buster Keaton running from crazed people after his hide. Buster Keaton never showed signs of being out of breath. Boo could feel the muscles around his stomach beginning to tense, cutting into required air capacity. A dog's hot breath filled the air, Boo swore those teeth were inches from his Achilles' heal.

The end of the driveway was close, but not close enough. From the east, a cloud of dust billowed like a dust bowl from the twenties. A lumbering sound of a passing Greyhound Bus caught Boo's ears, he began waving arms frantically at the passing bus. From the corner of the driver's eye she noticed the flagging of a potential passenger. Air brakes hissed, the bus tires bounced over ridges of hardened gravel until it swayed to a stop.

Head long into the cloud of dust engulfing the bus, Boo raced towards the opening door.

"Just in time my friend," blurted out a jolly woman of stature and humor, she quickly closed the door before the dust booked a free passage.

Boo coughed a reply, "Thank you, thank you."

"Take a seat sweetie, you can pay up when we reach the terminal." Into gear she set the bus into a forward motion.

Towards the back of the bus, Boo staggered on wobbly legs and a tightened chest. Sitting into a seat, he looked at the back of legs for teeth marks. Peeking out of the side window, Boo could see the figure of Irene waving from the front porch. People were staggering at different locations along the driveway. There at the end, by the rural route mail box, a big black dog sat with one paw clawing at the air. Boo waved back out of courtesy.

"Thanks for forcing me to run dog."

CHAPTER 8
BAR ROOM QUEENS

For most of the morning, Salami spent driving through the main parts of downtown Winnipeg. To him, all streets looked the same. By mid-morning, Salami knew he was lost. Where should he look, the downtown area, the up-town section or maybe the hospitals.

No-matter where Salami drove, people would stop what they were doing and gaze. Arrows where still intact and visible to onlookers. All Salami could do at the moment was to keep searching for Boo. There was no time to repair the truck at the moment.

Like any big city, heavy traffic entered the city limits on highways from other destinations. From all parts of the country, people traveled to metropolises by means of planes, trains, cars and buses. Winnipeg was no different than any other city. It was advantageous for Boo to arrive into the heart of the city on a Greyhound bus.

Lulled into a semi sleep by the hum of the Greyhound's motor, Boo dreamed of farmers toting shotguns and running after buses. When sleep waned, the bus was making its way to the downtown core, Boo was relieved to count seven similar Greyhound buses heading towards the terminal. Suddenly Boo stiffened with a Deja vu expression on a tired face. Peeking over the back seat, out through the tinted back window, Boo expected to see Little Abner hillbillies driving cut-down 1949 half ton trucks. Boo had hoped to see Irene's loving green eyes.

Without Boo's knowledge, the Greyhound bus did not head directly into Winnipeg that day. While Boo longed for needed sleep the bus headed to outlaying towns before circling back to Winnipeg twenty hours later, the next day. Unaware of the elapsing time, Boo was not attentive to the fact that Irene's father and kin had followed a bus later that morning. After the failed shotgun wedding, the men folk climbed into their trucks and headed onto the highway searching for the getaway bus, but which Greyhound bus.

"There's the bus!" yelled Buck from the trucks open box. "There's another one, Uncle Josh. I like riding in a big Greyhound Bus." Buck began to talk to himself. "All the way to Calgary to see the stampede."

Jock began counting the buses on the main city street leading towards the terminal. "Which one do you think it could be, Josh? There are about a dozen. They all look the same to me."

"All of them." Josh's anger seemed to be a hatred towards all Greyhound buses. "They are all heading to the main terminal. That Boo-bugger, has to get off one of them," confirmed Josh, his hands tightly gripping the steering wheel. "We will find the weasel there."

Three other trucks followed Josh, Jock and Buck, all willing and ready to avenge their family honor. A welcome-wagon of vigilantes. Where was Irene, was she well on her way out the back door, and slowly disappearing across the golden fields of wheat.

"Uncle Josh," informed a gleaming spiked haired Buck. "There is the Greyhound bus depot." Buck climbed in through the back window of the cab, squeezing between Josh and Jock. A shotgun rested between Buck's legs.

Josh observed the smiling kid. "We can not shoot him on sight." With a hand he leaned the shotgun towards the dashboard. "We are going to take him back to the farm. He is going to work, and if he does not work out to my satisfaction, then we shoot him."

Strange events happen all the time in a large city, and people seldom think anything of it. Events happen, then eventually fade away. For residents, it has become common place, as if there was live theater being performed during their daily lives. Live interaction without interaction for everyone waiting for the action of the day to begin. Having their morning coffee at a coffee shop across from the depot, two city cops waited for their cues.

Sam, a slightly over-weight cop, and his partner, Slim, noted for his tall slim frame, sat sipping the hot caffeine, as the players of life set the stage.

Slim pointed towards the depot. "Sam, did you see those fools drive into the bus terminal?"

"Yeah, probably justifiably late for their departing bus."

Scratching under the brim of a black cap, Slim pondered a thought. "When did the sidewalk beside the bus building become a parking lot?"

Sam did not look up from a large cup of black coffee. "Do not ask me, Slim." Sam glanced over. "Are you going to eat your doughnut today Slim?"

"Nah, go ahead. Too much sugar for me." Slim began to wonder if maybe something out of the ordinary was taking place across the street. Something dangerous, something involving firearms.

Without lifting his head, Sam dunked a glazed doughnut then savored it with his tongue.

"Rifles, Sam!"

"They are going hunting, and they are late for the bus."

Shaking his head in disagreement, Slim stirred the coffee with a straw. "I do not think so." Slim kept a curious eye on the carnival scene developing across the street.

Realizing that he had been on this street before, Salami began to look for familiar sights. "Yup, I was one this street, and that one," nodded Salami, with his head bobbing up and down like some cheap dashboard hula girl. "I turned that corner, up that street." Salami thought for a moment while waiting at a red light. "Big deal! I am still lost."

Deciding to turn down a side street, that he did not remember, Salami felt he was getting closer to a way out. Street people gawked, and chit-chat continued about the strange truck going around in circles, 'an oversized porcupine' was a common comment.

"Check those three buses over there," anger raged in the tone of Josh's voice. "And those two there."

From the inside of one of the buses, Boo crawled along the floor. After passing several seats, he would raise to peer out of a window. Boo was not concerned about the straggly look of his features reflecting from the tinted windows. Of importance was the sightings of those hillbillies wanting to abduct him.

Thinking that the bus was empty, Boo was startled when noticing old fashioned black nylon stockings covering short stubby legs dangling beneath a seat. On hands and knees, Boo slowly crawled towards the figure slumped in the seat. Peeking around the tattered seat corner, Boo viewed an elderly Granny fast asleep. In dreamland, she must be thinking of her visit to grand kids. Here on the bus, she was glad to have peace and quiet away from those over energized, ill mannered grand-children that she loved without malice.

Occupying the seat beside her was a lace hat and shawl. Covering her lap, a red and green checkered blanket rested, dainty hands rested funeral like on top. With a mischievous grin, Boo watched the little old lady slumber.

Stepping from the last step of the bus, a hunched over frame wobbled as she leaned on a crooked cane. Squeezing past, a chubby man and a little boy excused themselves for their haste. Boo mumbled something from beneath the veiled hat and shawl. Draped to the ground a green and red checkered blanket hid the wobbling legs of a scary looking grandmother. Raising the cane, Boo decided to refrain from striking at the kid that gave a repulsed glance back towards his poor imitation of an old lady.

Feeling foolish in the disguise, Boo hastened foot-work, dodging street vehicles in making an escape across the intersection. Car horns drew more attention than Boo had counted on. Having the speed of a sprinter beneath an old lady's attire, was sure to catch the eyes of pursuers.

Josh's eyes had been fixed on the old looking figure from the moment she had stepped from the bus. His presumptions were confirmed when Boo's leather boots flashed beneath the hanging blanket. "There he goes, across the street, the old lady."

Passer-byes stopped to look, Jock, Buck and the rest of the kin stopped to witness the strange lady.

"He is dressed like an old lady. After him you old fools," waved Josh as he yelled above the mid morning traffic. "What are you waiting for, an invitation?"

Several of the Watson clan pursued Boo, others blocked the street traffic to allow their trucks to make a U-turn.

Buck dodged the traffic holding the shotgun in both hands high above his head. "Stop Grandma, stop. Grandma."

"See, Slim, the crowd is breaking up." Sam leaned closer to his steaming cup of coffee.

"Those men are heading down the street after a little old lady. There have been no shots fired." noted Slim pushing his cap back to the crown of his head. "That little old lady has speed for her age."

"Slim, if you wait long enough, that whole event will go away." Sam began dunking the doughnut into the coffee without ever having raised his head to look out through the window.

Bit by bit, Boo discarded the hat, shawl and blanket as his speed increased. For the moment, Boo had a fair lead on intended in-laws.

Slamming on the brakes, Salami turned the steering wheel hard to the left, the tires squawked to a stop. "What the hell," commented Salami to himself. "What the hell are those idiots doing?"

Salami let two of the four trucks horde past him before deciding to join the parade of gun toting farmers. Intuition, or the fact that Salami knew that if there was something strange going on, Boo would be in the middle of it. Salami took the chance by following the strangers.

"Turn right," Josh demanded of Jock. "That Boo guy cut across to the next block."

In the stalled traffic of downtown Winnipeg, Josh and his kin along with Salami darted their eyes ahead, searching. Josh knew he was seeking Boo. Salami hoped it would be Boo. From a lane-way, Boo emerged onto the sidewalk filled with tourists being lectured to by an over zealous guide. Both Salami and Josh noticed Boo penetrating through the slow moving group of aged citizens. Salami was the quicker of the two to react. Boo's porcupine truck edged out then in-front of the farmers. Laying a fist onto the horn, Salami swerved the truck to straddle the sidewalk.

Jock pumped the breaks of the old truck as he tried to refrain from using profanity. "Do these heathens of this sinful city know how to drive."

"Put your dam foot on the gas pedal and follow him," said Josh to his brother, in a tone un-characteristic for a God-fearing man. "After that bastard."

"Please, please, everyone move to the side," announced a curly haired tourist guide. With fidgeting arms, he motioned for the German tourists to get out of the way. "Hug the building. Hug, hug," for emphases, the guide slapped arms around himself and waved the group towards the building.

Slowing his pace down, Boo turned to see his old faithful truck lumbering towards him. With a step up, Boo grabbed the side mirror and rested his foot on the wooden running boards. While Salami bounced the truck over the curb, he made a right turn onto a clear side street, Boo headed headfirst into the open window. Resting downward with long lanky legs resting on Salami and the steering column, the boys exchanged pleasantries.

"How have you been, Boo?"

"Not bad, yourself?"

"Just fine, thanks."

A heavy foot pressed the gas pedal until the Ford truck coughed up more speed. At this point in time, Boo wanted plenty of distance between him and disgruntled would-be in-laws.

Suzie was becoming board with the family's planed vacation. From the beginning everything was against her. The bathing suit she wanted, to not being able to visit the sights of Winnipeg. Some vacation, most of the time it was rush here then there. It seemed that her father's idea of a vacation was to spend it cooped up in a station-wagon speeding down another highway. Canada's scenery was a blur, evidence enough by the way her father drove. It was as if he wanted to finish their vacation in half the allotted time.

"Reese, it has been a long day," said Mrs. Roberts to her husband. "I think we should stop for the night. Everyone is getting a little restless."

Reese grumbled a bit, but he knew that his wife was right. "Yes fine. We will stop for the night in Regina," his words garbled as he spoke.

Under the scorching sun, by the middle of the afternoon, everyone in an un-air-conditioned vehicle was seeking a cool encampment. Along the endless flat-lands, the comfort of shade was a lost commodity. There was no exception for the Roberts, as they sought protection under cool shade trees by a rippling brook. A roadside campground, with trees of sparse leaf coverage and a pipe emitting water from the ground, would be their oasis.

Reese had other things in mind when he decided to stop at this luxury haven. Leaving the family to fend for themselves, Reese wandered off towards the main entrance and a single telephone booth. Slipping change into the coin slot, Reese began dialing long distance numbers. In a whispering voice, as if to hide, he asked the operator to connect him to the following extension.

"Yes, extension four, five, three, five." Reese glanced around to make sure no one was within hearing distance.

"Your number please.?"

"Four, five, three, five."

"What extension do you wish me to connect you with?"

Placing a cupped hand around the mouth piece, Reese raised a dry voice. "Four, five, three, five."

"Please go ahead."

"Hello, hello Fred, Reese here."

Wasting no time with pleasantries, Reese began to exchange information with his telephone counterpart. From the beginning Reese's story began to unravel. Plans for the upcoming days were hatched. As Reese spoke, Fred was becoming more excited, almost exhilarated to intoxication.

"We should be there by tomorrow afternoon," added Reese, as sweat gathered abundantly across a furrowed forehead. "Keep your eyes pealed for the truck, you can not miss it."

"You bet Reese. I will turn them into pulp."

"Wait until I get there. If you see them, track them."

Each said goodbye with a sinister smirk on their faces. Neither one could wait to inflict pain on Salami and Boo. Reese may have had reason, but what was Fred's provocation. Wiping the sweat from his forehead, Reese then wiped it against flowered shorts. A day's drive away, Fred was grinding a hardened fist into a callused palm.

A six-six, two hundred and sixty pound brother-in-law was a formidable weapon to have backing a sniveling man like Reese. Fred worked as a butcher more out of pleasure, which showed on his face when he worked.

Heading in a westerly direction, Salami and Boo exchanged experiences with a conscious fear. At odd moments, one or the other would turn to see if they were being pursued. Having originally planned on a trip west for the pleasure of having fun seemed like a great idea. Circumstances of having fun lead to trouble following their every step. Reese, cops, farmers. Why could it not be the hassle of having women after them. For whatever reason, someone wanted a piece of their hide.

"I do not have the answer Salami." Boo stretched legs and yawned.

"Boo," Salami began to say. "If we stay ahead of them, we will be fine." Salami eased the truck onto a bypass.

Under the harmonies of singers on a tape, injected into the tape player, the fields of wheat under a golden sunset began to set the boy's thoughts at ease. Into the darkening horizon the boys pushed on. Behind them, the sky was aglow above the refection of city lights, a beacon in the night. This night the lure of big city lights would entice someone else.

Stretches of highway, as straight as one's sight, let the Ford half ton cruse at a fast speed. When driving became too tedious, Salami pulled to the side of the road into a cluster of apple trees. Miles away from past trouble, the boys longed for sleep. Morning would find them two provinces away from Manitoba near the town of Medicine Hat Alberta.

Before the eight o'clock breakfast bell, Reese was up and at it with a destination in mind. No nagging wife or whining children was going to hold him back. Though hungry and tired, the Roberts climbed into the heat infested station-wagon, to make up traveling time, along the Trans Canada highway.
In Medicine Hat, Reese's brother-in-law was out on the highway by six in the morning. A bird dog waiting for the early bird. Fred chewed chunks of dried beef jerky clenched in massive fist.

Of the four farmers trucks, there now were only two on the road. Though less vehicles, the number of passengers had increased. Kinfolk were loaded like upright cordwood in the open box of the trucks. There was no doubt that the would-be bride was well on her way, even though the irrational men folk were still seeking a groom for Irene, and a farm hand for Josh Watson. To keep their eyes open, for the search of the maroon truck with sticks sticking out of it, Josh turned on the C.B.C radio station.
"Back in Ontario, the small town of Wawa is still in the news. Police there are searching for two men that have defaced the town goose, a statue of a Canada Goose. In Marathon, the O.P.P. had one suspect in custody, but he escaped with a bankroll that was being held in transit. Native uprising, into it's second week outside of Dryden Ontario. Local police noticed a truck fitting the description of the one sought by Wawa O.P.P., they did not give chase. Last seen heading west on Seventeen."

Suzie sat quietly in the back seat of the family's station-wagon. So far, this trip had been a complete waste of her anticipated enjoyment. This time in Medicine Hat, she vowed not to let the past happen again. Suzie was going to make a point of doing the things she wanted to do, her way. With Tina, her cousin, they were going to let loose and really live.
After corresponding with each other for the past eight years, both had planned to visit the other, but each time, it had to be postponed. This time, this summer, they would not let circumstances stop their plans.

With a daydream smile on her face, Suzie laid out plans for herself and Tina. As soon as they arrived in Medicine Hat, Tina and herself would take what they needed for the beach and the night life. In Tina's 63 M.G. they would take off, leaving the kids and old folks at home. Returning home would only occur when they tired of the carefree life.

Suzie felt that they were old enough, in an innocent way, to taste life's sweet and bitter wines. If only to experience life to the limit.

Tagging behind, the family's trailer followed the station-wagon without complaint. Inside of the station-wagon it was not much different. No-one spoke much, each seemed to be in their own little world. For some time, Mrs. Roberts noticed that Reese had something on his mind, something was bothering him since they were in Winnipeg. When she tried to confront him, he would say it was nothing, and that he would take care of it.

'Take care of what,' she thought. 'What had he to take care of. Was this something to do with his hurrying to get from one place to another?' She was afraid to ask him about it, she was worried. 'Here is not the place or time to start an argument.' covering her mouth, Mrs. Roberts pondered this strange vacation.

Reese glanced into the rear-view mirror to see Al and Mary playing some card game together. Suzie sat smiling as she stared out through the side window. Peeking to his right side, Reese noticed his wife deep in thought. 'Probably thinking about what I am up to,' Thought Reese. 'Well, she will just have to put up with it until I have done what I need to do.'

"We will be in Medicine Hat in about two hours," informed Reese to his wife and brood. This, he had thought, would get the boredom off their minds, relieving him from having to answer questions.

"That is fine Dear," softly replied Mrs. Roberts, without removing her chin resting on an upturned hand.

For AL and Mary, the news was something to jump up in their seats about. Suzie just decreased the time required before she and Tina would disappear into their own world.

Visions of gun toting in-laws and a fleeing bride to-be dwelled in Boo's panic stricken dream world. Sprawled across the front seat, Boo's legs fought to be freed from the clutches of the steering wheel.

Under the mid day sun, Boo slumped out of the truck to the dry ground beneath the apple trees. Salami offered a cool tasting apple to his friend. There was no one chasing them, so why the need to flee. Without words, the two road weary fellows leaned back against the trees, devouring the free meal. Salami pointed to a place name on the road map. Nodding in agreement, Boo read the name of Medicine Hat

'Maybe tonight,' both thought. 'In the cool of the evening we might visit the town.'

"They are here!" yelled Tina, from the front door of their hardboard clad house. "They are finally here."

Fred, wife and three other small children watched Reese's car pull into the driveway. A lumbering dinosaur of a vehicle sighed to a stop. Dancing in each other's arms, Tina and Suzie hugged and kissed with non-sequential words floating into each other's ears. Hellos were brief for the two girls as they quickly drifted away.

Like the girls, Fred and Reese stood aside while the wives and kids did the family thing. Reese sought information.

With a somber voice, Reese asked. "Did you see the truck and those two guys I described to you?"

A nod of Fred's head urged Reese to walk to the opposite side of the driveway. "I was out on the main highway at six this morning." Fred rubbed a bloodshot eye. "I did not see a sign of those guys. They did not come through this morning."

Fred and Reese were busy, the kids were off playing, the women were caught up in the latest gossip to notice Tina and Suzie packing their belongings into the back of the M.G.

No-one paid attention to their departure.

"Fred," Reese began to act as a foreman, giving out orders. "First, we will set up the trailer, then plan on where we are going to go to look for those guys." Reese stopped walking, he stopped rubbing a whiskered chin. "They might have stopped some place for the night, planning to travel later today."

"Maybe," Fred answered with a questionable voice. "Are you sure they are coming this way?"

"I am sure," Reese's voice sounded with confident assurance. "They have to come this way."

Boo added another apple core to an apple core pile. Reclining beneath the tree gave time for thought reassessment.

"Salami, this trip was suppose to be just plain fun. A few women and a few good times."

"It has been Boo." Salami rested on elbows. "I have had a good time, you?"

"Some," answered Boo. "What about Reese, the cops in Wawa and Marathon and those farmers. They were not carrying pee-shooters."

"Ah shucks!" laughed Salami at the predicament. "As long as we stay ahead of them, we are laughing."

"Ahead of them. They have to catch us first." Boo began pulling boots on after a needed stretch. 'What if they catch us.' thought Boo. 'Then what do we do?'

Rocking back and forth on the ground, Salami scratched his back against the exposed roots of the apple tree. "Ahh . . .."

"Time to move Salami, lets make like we are out of here."

Left behind to savor in it's own peacefulness, the apple grove waited for the next seeker of nourishment and relaxation. Reluctantly, the Ford truck crept back onto the highway heading towards Medicine Hat.

Rays of golden beams played tag among the fields of wheat. A pungent smell of barley mixed with the sweet aroma of granola floated freely on the warm streams of prairie air. A haze of Mother nature's scents lingered close to the ground level, an earthly smell. Only an outsider would turn a nose away, thinking of the bouquet as foul.

Tina's red M.G. was noticed by more than a few people. Mostly guys cruising with nothing better to do then search for women to fantasize about. Hungry stares were attracted by the hot little car with maturing adolescent riders. Cruising up and down the sleepy prairie town's main street, Tina searched for a place to park. Parking in a prominent spot was the social ritual of coming of age.

Being cousins from different parts of the country does not always mean that cousins, of the same age and height, may not resemble each other. After all, their mothers were sisters. Tina and Suzie stood five six, both wore their light brown hair straight and to the shoulders. Other than a slightly darker tan that Tina had, their resemblance was close to that of twins. Their development into shapely young ladies could only be enhanced by their modest weight.

"Two for the price of one," yelled a voice in the crowd, making the rounds of the main street.

Leather attired bikers made their presence known. "Double the pleasure."

Groups of young, and not so young stood gathered with their own kind. High-school football players stood huddled together with female groupies around their fringes. Men past their teen years paraded around in tight tee-shirts, flexing muscles that were developed for only show. The group that held everyone's attention, demanded attention, were the bikers wearing their colours.

"Over here sweetheart!" called out another biker, trying to gain the girls' attention. "We aim to please."

"This is the town?" asked Suzie, looking up and down the street. "This is it?" Her eyes drifted from one group to another.

"It is home for now." Tina lifted herself onto the lip of the car door. "I do not plan on being here forever."

Following Tina's move, Suzie sat up onto her door, loosening her blouse to reveal a bikini top. In the dry warm air, she dared to reveal more. In this gathering of people, she was the most modest in attire. Yearning eyes of men ventured towards the girls. Other girls and women smirked at the intruding competition. One group eyed another group with disdain, yet afraid to approach the girls.

Tina opened her blouse to reveal an even skimpier top. "I thought your mother would not let you buy a bikini?"

Looking wide eyed at Tina's top, Suzie replied, "Not one as skimpy as yours. I managed to buy this one in Winnipeg when I had a chance to shop behind my mother's back."

"Tina leaned closer to whisper, "Well, do not show too much."

A prairie afternoon leading into a colourful evening sky held no interest for the two girls. Only the talk of the other's experiences, boys, school and the chance to get out into the world held their immediate attention. Though the red M.G., and themselves, held the attraction of the various groups of men, the girls paid them no mind.

Noticing a biker with a beer in his hand strolling in their direction, Tina decided it was time to move. "Suzie, it is time to see some other sights." Sliding down into the seat, Tina pressed the clutch as she turned the ignition key. "One of those bikers is getting too interested in us."

Curiosity held Suzie's interest. Looking around to see the man in question, Suzie held onto the front wind-shield frame and seat as the M.G. roared to life. Clipping the curb onto the street, the little red car seemed to speed away faster because of it's sleekness. Standing disillusioned, the biker guzzled the beer and scratched at his groin with an idle hand.

Warm wind tossed the girl's hair wildly in the open M.G.. Scooting along a secondary highway, laughter was carried away across the fields. What two girls had to talk about seemed endless. They paid no notice to their surroundings, or events that occupied the same point in time.

An occasional glance into the rear-view mirror revealed an assembly of motorcycles reducing the distance between them. Tina's facial expression implied a concern to Suzie. "Whoops."

Suzie held her hair to the side of her face. "What is the matter?" asked Suzie leaning sideways to look at the cars gauges. "Are you running out of gas?"

"Oh no, just that, I think those bikers are following us."

Suzie flirted with danger while she began to tease Tina. Vamp-like, she loosened her blouse, tilted her head back and forced her chest upward. "Slow down, see what they want."

"Suzie, you can not do that. Cover yourself." Tina griped the small steering wheel. Maintaining a constant speed, she concentrated on staring straight ahead. Girl talk for the moment ceased.

Suzie was quick to cover herself when the roar of bikes edged closer. Sinking into the seat seemed to be a good idea. "Do you think that maybe you should drive a little faster, like lose them."

With the roar appearing to get louder, Tina began to slow down. Pulling up along the driver's side, a tall clean shaven man slightly smiled to Tina. Suzie was not as privileged; her view was of a long-bearded guy with a red tongue lapping at scared lips. Suzie had to see what was following. Swallowing, she turned to see a three-wheel trike carrying two females caressing their chests. They threw kisses of invitation.

"Looking for a good time, children?" implied the dirty looking bearded biker. "You have found it."

A strong glare passed from Suzie to Tina, as the clean biker spoke to Tina. "Do not take Hog literally," said the biker as he down shifted the Harley. "Hog gets that way the first day he gets out of the pen."

Tina tried to smile with confidence. The wrong thing to do was to give the car a burst of speed, which she did. Inevitable, was the bikers doing the same.

"The name is Hooker," the man said, after the chatter of the bike's burst of speed left the exhaust pipe. "Do you have a name?"

Tina did not answer; her reply was a raised eye-brow and a shrug of shoulder. Suzie avoided looking at the one called Hog. Holding hair from the left side, she turned to notice another biker behind the trike. A younger looking guy with a drooping mustache, long and bushy, draping the cute corners of his lips. Suzie returned his awkward smile.

Without thinking, Suzie had become intrigued. Leaning in-front of Tina she asked the leader. "What is the cute guy's name?" Suzie surprised herself with her forwardness.

Hooker turned to see a faint smile vanish from his younger brother's face. "That's Speed, Snow and Coke on the trike. Hog over there and that is Henry in the rear."

"Henry," Suzie gave a disappointed glare when she repeated the name. 'He is still good looking,' she thought.

Henry pulled out from behind the trike edging up behind Hooker. He did not fit the image of a biker. It was as if he was there with rough and rumbling members because he looked up to his brother. On occasion Henry glanced across towards Suzie.

"Your names?" asked Hooker. "You do have names?"

Tina forced a fake smile, as she clutched the M.G. into gear. "We have to meet people at the next stop. Bye." A burst of gas propelled a blur of the red car down the highway.

Familiar sounds of choppers rattled with acceleration. Giving chase after the girls, the bikers tore up the highway. At a leisurely pace they followed, keeping the little car in sight. On long straight stretches of highway it was not difficult to see an object three miles away.

In the middle of nowhere, a long low building sat by its self on the side of the highway. A watering hole in modern times for road weary travelers. A bar, restaurant, and night club where country bands are the norm. Tina had been to the bar several times this summer after turning legal age. Pulling into this place was the safe thing to do at the moment. Here, there were plenty of people around with bouncers that were ex- college wrestlers.

Dry dust billowed as Tina's car creped into the dirt parking lot. Rustic barn board covered the exterior of the windowless bar. Barn style doors with a sign overhead was the only indication that this was a bar. On a two by four-foot sign, in simple block letters it stated that this place was, 'Joe's Bar and Grill'.

Hurrying to enter the bar, Tina and Suzie looked back up the highway to see how close the bikers were behind them. In relief they noticed nothing through the dissipating dust. Giggles of comfort came in small bursts from the girls, as they entered the bar and grill.

Smoke filled the dimly lit bar, at this time of day, it was just beginning to fill with hungry and thirsty patrons. Both girls moved about slowly until their eyes adjusted to the lack of light. Finding a small empty table to the side, they sat down, letting out long breaths. Relaxation for the moment.

"What will it be?" asked an elderly waitress standing by the table, her aurora lacking patience.

"Draft," replied Tina. "Suzie what are you having?"

Suzie had never had the experience before. Faking her experience she answered. "The same please."

Girl talk continued through sips of draft beer. Country classics boomed from the juke-box. Hard luck and sappy sentimental songs placed the customers in a solace mood. A mood that seemed to make customers order more drinks to enhance their happiness or drown their sorrows. Either way, Joe of Joe's bar and Grill was happy.

Comfortable in their own world, the girls did not notice the bikers enter the bar and grill until they loomed over the table with beers in their hands.

Hooker politely asked, "May we join you?"

Hog did not wait for an invitation, he pulled a chair up and sat between Tina and Suzie. It was too late for the girls to react. Gripping their hands around their draft glasses, they endured the biker's presence with forced grimaces. Taking a chair and turning it backwards, Hooker sat on it close to Tina. A shy Henry sat a step back but close to Suzie. Both Henry and Suzie avoided direct contact between their eyes.

There was a satisfaction that the girls were pleased about. Speed, Snow and Coke sat at another table looking disgusting. Hog rested a huge arm close to Suzie, his glare was repulsive. Henry backed up his chair to make room for Suzie to move away. Their eyes met then shyly turned away.

"This is a nice-looking place," noted Henry. "Nice."

Hog and Hooker stared dumfounded at Henry, for saying such an inappropriate comment for a biker.

"We have been traveling for hours," Josh said to Jock and Buck, sitting beside him in the truck. "We have not seen any sign of that pin cushion of a truck."

Jock turned a tired head to Josh. "They can not be too far ahead of us. Maybe only an hour behind them."

Josh eased up on the gas. "It could be that they are not ahead of us."

Looking straight forward into the darkening sky, Josh rolled thoughts over in his mind. Buck was losing his grin of excitement. Suddenly, Josh brought the truck to a screeching stop. Bodies in the back box piled together. From the second truck could be heard the locking up of tires as the headlights stopped inches from the tailgate of the front truck. In back, the kinfolk were wrapped as tight as friendly sardines.

"They knew we were going to follow them," spoke Josh, peering at a point in the distance. "They stopped someplace to hide. There was a town we passed by."

"Seven Persons, no Medicine Hat, they stopped to hide there," added Jock. "Medicine Hat is a bigger town to hide in."

"Right," agreed Josh. Pulling hard on the cracked steering wheel, Josh attempted a sharp and quick U-turn.

Buck suddenly emitted a broad smile of anticipated excitement. When the trucks lurched forward, the kin in the back of the trucks piled into a close-knit family.

"Boo, right there." Salami pointed to the side of the road. "Joe's Bar and Grill."

"No need to look further." Boo turned the truck into the parking lot filled to the limit. "I do not think there is a need to seek out the competition, Joe's place has the market cornered." Backing the truck bumper to bumper with a little red car, Boo turned off the ignition.

Salami and Boo stood outside of the truck looking in all directions. As far as the eye could see, there were no lights from other establishments or town buildings.

"This place looks like the best place to be," confirmed Salami, as Boo nodded with agreement.

Salami forced hands through curly blonde hair in an effort to comb it. He gave up, deciding to adjust clothes instead. From behind the seat, Boo withdrew a clean denim shirt with bucking horses stitched across the front.

"The place looks safe," said Boo.

Salami checked the highway up and down. "This place is on a secondary highway, and out in the middle of nowhere."

"Trouble seems to follow us." Boo paused at the barn doors, as he held it open for his buddy. "I think we create trouble."

"Lets just be observers tonight."

Squinting to see through the darkness of dim yellow lights and dark red walls, Boo and Salami waded through a sawdust floor towards the bar.

"No-one will notice us in here, it is too dam dark." Boo leaned against the oiled maple lip of the bar.

Ordering from the chalk board menu, Boo ordered a steak sandwich and a pitcher of cold water. Beer and a hot sausage sandwich was Salami's idea of wholesome food fair. Boo asked the bar maid to take the order to the far end of the bar. At that end, where it was darker, the band members gathered with their followers. There, Boo and Salami could keep their backs to the wall, and their eyes covering the rest of the bar, just in case.

Through the afternoon and into the early evening hours, Reese and Fred had staked out an intersection leading into town. Eyes searched the horizon for a glimpse of Boo's truck. Wasted hours passed without a sign, or a clue of where their quarry was.

"It is getting late Reese," informed Fred, turning up the collar of his shirt. A cool breeze from the northwest tickled his neck. "They could have passed through late last night or early this morning."

"No, no, no-way. You did not see them this morning, and I did not see them on our way in." Reese spat several times until the shreds of cigar left his mouth. "They had to stop somewhere for the night." Moving to the front of the grey Jeep, Reese moved eyes across the horizon. "They will be coming this way. In the night, they will make their move." Reese spat as he talked to Fred. "Tonight."

'Obsession,' was what Fred was thinking of Reese. Reese was preoccupied with revenge. How bad did he want to hurt those fellows? If it was anything like the way Reese murdered an inanimate cigar, heaven help them. Yes, Fred had agreed to back Reese up, but this waiting was beyond his patience. Television wrestling was on at ten. Joining Reese at the front of the Jeep, Fred waited impatiently.

One of the band members handed a sheet of paper to Salami. "It is open night. Anyone interested in singing or playing, sign up then pass the sheet along."

"Sure," said Salami passing it directly to Boo.

Jotting his name down, Boo then handed it onto another table then watched it float from table to table. Looking over the information, Hooker asked the others if any one wanted to sign. Heads shook and he passed it along.

"I guess no one is musically inclined." Hooker looked at Hog. "We all know that Hog plays tunes through his back-end. We should sign him up."

Being in the company of the bikers was not all that terrible. Embarrassing at times when brash language and gestures arose. Suzie was sheltered from this type of conduct, she lacked the ability to cope. Surely, Tina did not want to get too deeply involved with these strange men. What good times the girls were exploring was not the same as these bikers. History or the way the image of the biker has been portrayed is a different definition of fun.

Hog's attempts to satisfy his need to touch the soft flesh of Suzie's arm brought rejection. Suzie twitched away. Henry moved his chair closer to Hooker, giving Suzie room to move. Soon one side of the table was becoming crowded, leaving Hog to stretch out arms on the other side.

Both girls looked at each other with a shared thought and said, "We have to go water the Lilies." Standing, the girls smirked at the coincident of what they had said.

Hooker touched Tina's arm, startling her. "Hurry back, and do not drown the Lilies."

Once inside of the washroom, Tina leaned against the door holding it closed. "I feel like a pet dog sitting between those two guys."

"Henry is cute," Suzie replied.

"What about the other Neanderthals?" Tina shivered at the thought of getting close to a biker. "Hooker is not all that bad, but he is hovering too close to me."

"Tina, these guys are not our type."

"Yeah, I know. We should get out of here, somehow. Without them following us."

Suzie tapped a foot anxiously. "Tina, I really have to pee."

"Then pee while I think of something." Tina began to pace in front of the stalls, talking as she walked. "Escorts, we need someone to escort us out of here. That is it. When we see someone single, not too weird, near the dance floor, we get up and ask them to dance."

"Ask strangers to dance?"

"Sure, then we get them to escort us out."

"What happens when the bikers come after us?"

"Our escorts confront them, then they start a shoving match, then a fight breaks out, and we sneak away scot-free," said Tina, while brushing hair with an air of confidence.

"Right, just like in the movies." Suzie did not seem to share in the plausibility of this plan working without a hitch.

Entering the room from the bright light of the washroom, the girls stood by the bar.

"Stay on this side of the room." Tina began to lead Suzie along the bar towards the dance floor. "Remember, when we see someone, ask him to dance."

Suzie replied with a nod.

"Our second entertainer of the night," announced the lead singer of the band. "is a cowboy named Boo. Give him a hand."

Boo acknowledged the slight round of applause as he took to the stage. Adjusting a borrowed guitar and testing the mike, Boo introduced the song to the audience. "This song is for all the girls named Sally. Do we have anyone named Sally here tonight?"

"Here, over here, one over here," called out several voices in the dark.

Raising a hand to block the stage lights, Boo tried to locate the voices and the faces of the girls named Sally. Boo strummed Several chords to get a feel for the guitar and sound. "Then, this song goes out to you."

Tina pointed. "Suzie over there. That guy at the end of the bar with the curly blonde hair."

"Okay, go for it. I will wait here." Suzie nudged Tina to move as the beat of the song gave an intro to the style of song.

Behind Boo, the band quickly found the feel to the song and picked up the pace of a fast 4/4 bluegrass style song.

"This one is called 'Sally Gee'," announced Boo.

"No, no," protested Tina. "Wait for a slow song so we can be close enough to talk to him." Tina backed further behind a building support post. Bluegrass sounding music filled the bar.

Where're you going Sally May,
Where're you going so far from the mill.
She said, I'm going blue berry picking,
On the far side of the hill.
You sweet boy.
You sweet toy.

Can I tag along with you,
Can I walk with you this one time,
She said, only if you promise,
That you will always be mine,
You sweet thing.
You sweet thing.

Blue berry picking with Sally,
We never do no picking you see,
A good ole girl is Sally,
Picking berries with Sally Gee.

Your Mama Gee would say child,
Ain't no berries picked at all today,
Oh Ma, I must have dropped them,
All along the way.
Yes I did,
Yes I did.

And who were you with girl,
That scrawny ole kid they call chicken?
Momma's gonna whip you,
You ain't been picking,
No you weren't,
No you weren't.

Blue berry picking with Sally,
We never do no picking you see,
A good ole girl is Sally,

Picking berries with Sally Gee.

Sally took my hand,
Sally Gee touched my knee,
Sally Gee shouted out loud,
Do you want me?
Yes I do,
Yes I do.

Sally is a good girl,
Sally is good you see,
I'm gonna take Sally home,
Yes home with me.
Yes I am,
Yes I am.

Picking berries with Sally Gee.

After arousing applause, filled with hoots from the girls, the band slowed things down with a slower song. Boo accepted the adulation, as he stepped down from the stage into the shadows of the stage lights. Tina and Suzie peered out from behind the post looking for someone or something.

"There, over there is a guy getting up," Suzie said to Tina. "Go and ask him to dance."

Tina hesitated. "I have never had to ask a guy to dance."

"There is always a first time." Suzie gave Tina a gentle shove with a push of force.

Ending up on the dance floor, unable to turn back, Tina reluctantly sauntered towards a guy standing by the edge of the hardwood dance floor.

Unaware that he was a suspect, Salami was only heading to the men's room by way of crossing the dance floor. Before reaching the opposite side of the floor, a beautiful girl out of nowhere griped his arm with determination.

"Let's dance," boldly and with much too much forwardness, Tina suggested. "You do like to dance?" Tina took Salami's hand in hers and rested her other on his shoulder.

Salami was surprised, but intrigued, he took full advantage of the situation. Questions could be asked at a later moment. 'Who needs to answer questions,' thought Salami. 'I do not need to ask too many questions.'

Boo had noticed two girls acting agitated when he was on stage. Stepping into the darkness, he saw only the shadow of one girl hiding, it seemed, behind a support post. He had nothing to lose by approaching the shy looking girl.

Salami leaned his head closer to his dance partner, surely expecting the girl to back away. To Salami's surprise, Tina leaned closer also, but with a different intention.

Whispering into his ear, Tina began to say, "I need some help. We have to get out of here. Will you help us?"

Continuing to dance without really interpreting what was said, Salami just enjoyed the closeness. Two warm bodies close together. "Sure, I will," answered Salami without absorbing the depth of the plea for help.

"There are four guys over there that we were sitting with." Tina tried to lead Salami on the dance floor towards the farthest side, away from the bikers. "They look pretty mean."

Looking casually at the silhouettes of different shadows of people throughout the bar, Salami nodded his head as if agreeing. "No problem." Salami attempted a kiss to Tina's neck. "No problem at all."

"Stop, if those guys see you doing that, they will probably break your lips," Tina's voice rose. "I did not ask you to put your slobbering lips on my neck."

"Break my lips. Oh no, not that!" Salami began to tease. "Not my lips, I need my lips," said Salami, continuing to kiss the sweaty softness of Tina's neck. When given the opportunity, Salami had to give all efforts a try.

"Hey Hooker, some guy is moving in on your chick," informed Hog, standing to point towards Tina and Salami on the dance floor. "That guy, fresh off the farm, is kissing her neck."

Turning, Hooker's eyes flared with hate. "Where is the little pig?"

Standing up on a chair, Hog pointed with both hands to the opposite side of the dance floor. "There they are."

"That little runt!" pushing away the chair with the back of his legs, Hooker stood and entered onto the dance floor. With flaying arms, a path was cleared of dancers. Hooker made his way towards Tina and Salami.

Hog began jumping up and down on the chair seat, yelling encouragement to the biker leader, "Get that little runt. Carve him up."

Backtracking from the west, two trucks headed towards Medicine Hat. Tired and angry farmers filled the truck boxes. Overworked engines gave off the smell of burnt oil. On the main streets of the small city, the trucks drove two abreast as its occupants viewed the sidewalks and side streets. They were interested in anything that looked suspicious, anything that resembled a truck with arrows sticking out of it's body.

Passing from one end of town to the other, found the farmers no luckier. They were no closer to Boo then they had been the day before. Stopping in the middle of the street, side by side, the truck's occupants looked at each other dumb-founded.

Blank faces of Jock and Buck faced Josh, as if to say, 'what now'. Without saying a word, Josh drove the truck slowly forward in a direction out of town. Headlights mixing with the semi darkness did not illuminate much along the sides of the highway. What did grab Josh's attention was the figures of two men leaning against a battered looking Jeep. Changing gears as he double clutched, Josh slowed the truck to a stop.

Sticking his head out of the window, Josh called out to the two men, "Evening."

Reese and Fred returned the gesture promptly, "Evening."

Josh got right to the point saying, "Have you two been waiting here long?"

A glance of reluctance flowed between Reese and Fred. Reese spoke up first after taking a finger to wipe away tobacco juice from lips, "Oh I would not say we have been here all that long."

Buck began to say something, but Josh quickly reached back with an elbow to silence the kid. "Did you happen to notice," Josh asked slowly being careful of his words. "a red or wine coloured truck with . . ., sticks sticking out all over it?"

Fred uttered the start of a word as he raised a hand. Reese quickly interrupted before Fred said something substantial. "Cannot say that we have. No, no, not the past hour." Reese pretended to act innocent. "Was there one or two guys in this, this red truck. Were they heading east or west?"

135

Josh knew he was answering too quickly, but the words had left his mouth. "Two guys and they were heading west the last time we saw them." Josh scratched at day old growth of beard that showed whiter than he wished for.

Pulling then scratching under his belt, where the flab of his stomach rested, Reese hid the fact that the information was of importance to him. "No," answered Reese with a thinking sway of his head. In Reese's mind, thoughts were being pieced together.

Buck mumbled something to Josh that Reese could not hear, but that did not stop him from stepping closer to the truck. Maybe the kid had said something of importance .

"What was that. The kid needs to ask something?" Reese looked Josh directly into the eyes.

"Ah," Josh delayed answering, as he thought of a diversion. "The kid here wants to know if there is a place around here to eat. A hamburger joint or something?"

Pointing down a side road, Fred answered, "Joe's Bar and Grill. A mile or so east."

Josh put the steaming truck into gear. Passive thanks he gave to Reese and Fred as he and kinfolk journeyed on, "Much obliged for the information."

Watching the two old farm truck's tail lights fading into the distance, Reese was putting two and two together. "They have to eat. Everyone has to eat." He spat tobacco juice, hitting the dry ground and staying in a ball. "Let's go Fred, follow them."

Salami seemed to be in seventh heaven as he nibbled on Tina's ear lobe. Holding him at bay did not seem to deter Salami.

"Stop that! I need help, not your affection." Tina turned her head away from Salami and glanced about the room.

"This is the way I affectionately help out," said Salami in a voice as romantic as he would ever be. Salami tasted his lips. "Not bad. Do you have a name?"

"Oh no, here he comes. We are going to receive pain." Tina pulled Salami closer to her warm body. She clung to him for protection, not for the thoughts floating through Salami's mind. "I told you, I had to get out of here, it is a matter of life and death."

Obviously, Salami was not listening. "Oh, that is better."

Hooker's boots clipped at every step, clipping above the sound of the music. Tina distinctively heard each step getting louder as

Hooker approached. As if tossing toothpicks, Hooker's hands tossed the local boys out of the way. A painful grip pinched Salami's shoulder, Hooker pulled him away from Tina. Before a massive fist contacted Salami's face, Tina gave Hooker a swift kick to the knee cap. Wincing with pain, Hooker still managed to lower a fist towards Salami. In that split second, a local boy, more the size of Hooker, caught the fist in the palm of a hand. Heads turned towards the sound of the slap.

Sweet slow waltz music from the band began to take on a faster tempo. Frantic commotion on the dance floor reflected in the mood of the musician's playing. The big local boy squeezed and twisted the arm of Hooker, bringing the biker to his knees. Hog stopped his jumping on the chair when he saw the tide of affairs changing. Summing Speed and Henry, the trio advanced across the dance floor.

Frenzied music blaring from the speakers agitated the emotions of patrons of Joe's Bar and Grill. Not to miss out on the action, a band member kicked over a mike stand just as Hog passed in front of the bandstand. Hog's head took the full impact of the mike. Feedback pierced through the bar adding sound effects to the scuffling taking place on the dance floor. Boo watched from the sidelines, not yet ready to lend Salami a hand. Suzie had given Boo interest of more importance. At the outset of the scuffle, Suzie grasped Boo's arm and hid behind his tall frame.

Before the bikers realized the quickness of the local boys, they found themselves surrounded. A bar style of kick ball was beginning. Local boys in a circle began to push the bikers from side to side. Like bingo balls in a tumbler, spinning, turning, bouncing aimlessly. Salami, holding onto Tina's hand, quickly escaped through the crowd to the safety outside of the center. Not being interested in the child's game, the girl bikers, Snow and Coke huddled together trying not to be noticed.

By now, the band was playing with gusto, the bar was hopping with hysteria. One of the local boys picked up the loose mike to begin wrapping the cord around Hog's neck. It was the mike that he shoved into Hog's mouth that sent loud gurgling sounds over the P.A. system. To make sure that hog stayed down, several others began to wrap the cord around his legs. Boo and Salami stood at different sides of the floor watching with interest at the strange ritual. Surely they were not the cause of this fiasco. They would, by way of default, be included.

Tina caught Suzie's attention by waving an arm. A jerk of her head sideways motivated the two to escape from this premise. Interested in the outcome of the culture clash on the dance floor, both Boo and Salami noticed that the clinging of girl's hands to their bodies had disappeared. The scent of a woman was more of a calling card then the brutality of a common brawl.

Each seeing their interest heading out of the bar, they quickly followed. At the same moment, Boo and Salami reached the exit door, each tried to force past the other.

"Salami, are you after the same girl as I am?" Boo forced himself through the door first.

"Light brown hair, shoulder length," informed Salami.

"Sounds familiar," said Boo, facing Salami.

"Hot, with a nice dark tan."

"No Tan," Boo clarified.

Even in the open spaces of the outdoors, the sounds of music and hyper voices penetrated through the bar's exterior walls. Standing there, Boo and Salami adjusted their eyes to the night, as they surveyed the parking lot for the disappearing girls.

"Did you start that commotion in there?" asked Boo politely.

"No." Salami studied Boo's eyes. "I thought that you did. Maybe they did not like that song of yours."

"Funny."

Standing at the side of the red M.G., the girls were perplexed at the thought that someone would have the nerve to block in their car at both the front and back.

"Hell!" stammered Tina, her feet stomping the dry hard dirt of Alberta.

Suzie fidgeted with the front of her blouse. "How in the hell are we going to get out of here. Those bikers are going to get kicked out of the bar, then they are going to come looking for us. I do not want to be standing here waiting. Tina?"

With both hands, Tina stroked them through her hair at the sides of a pounding head. "I am thinking."

Taking out her frustrations, Tina began to kick the bumper of the truck parked in front of her car. Suzie followed suit, adding pleasure to confound the seriousness of their situation.

"Shit, shit, shit!"

"Double Shit!" added Suzie.

Standing at the back of the M.G., Salami and Boo stood watching the girls kicking the crap out of the truck. Both shrugged their shoulders with amusement.

"Boo, I think my girl is kicking your Truck."

"AHHH !!!" echoed the startled girls, turning to face Boo and Salami.

"Salami, they do look alike," informed Boo. This one here." Boo pointed to Suzie. "No tan. I met her behind a post in the bar."

Gasping for breath, with hands pressed against their beating chests, the girls collapsed onto the bumper of the truck.

"The tanned one was all over me on the dance floor."

"Excuse me," Tina retaliated, standing, she quickly gave Salami a piece of her mind, "I was not all over you. I was asking you for your help. We needed to get away from some bikers sticking to us like day old fly paper."

"I thought she mumbled something while we were making out."

"We were not making out."

A rough introduction was made as to who was who, with an explanation as to why the girls wanted to leave in such a hurry. Tina seemed to express anxiety with a verbal tone.

"Mr. Boo, kindly move your truck so we can get out of here."

"I will tell you what." Boo looked at Tina as she stood swaying. "You are too nervous to drive, and you seem to be tipsy."

"So, I have had a few drinks."

"You and Salami ride together, and Suzie and I will test drive your nice bright red go-cart."

"Fine," answered Tina, slapping the car keys into Boo's hand. "As long as we get out of here."

"Ah!" Suzie began to say, but changed her mind, realizing that the longer they stayed, the likelihood that the bikers would be out to claim their women. "Let's go."

Salami and Tina rushed into Boo's truck. Suzie was seated in the M.G. while Boo attempted to squeeze his lanky frame into the pint sized car.

"We do not have all night," Suzie was adding to her nervousness as she constantly looked over a shoulder towards the bar's exit.

Roaring to a start, the M. G.'s engine emitted a distinctive sound. At the exit doors, the bikers were being escorted through the doors with a persuasive force. Their ears picked up the sound of the M.G.. Hooker picked himself up from the ground, dusting the dry dirt from leather pants.

Hog pulled at the cord around his legs. "What now Hooker?"

"After those two bar room Queens." There was a sinister appearance on his face, he was now humiliated. His only recourse was retribution. "I will deal with that guy with my fist."

By the time they rushed to start their bikes, the truck and M.G. had left the parking lot. Rattling engines and tires kicked up loose dirt. The bikers vacated the parking lot at full acceleration. Four choppers roared across the parking lot, over the grass divider to the hot asphalt of the secondary highway.

Headlights passed on the dark highway. Jock turned his head to catch the glimpse of arrows sticking out of a truck. Buck began to rock on the seat, a delighted sinister grin came to lips.

"That is the truck Josh," Jock said, informing Josh. "They just passed us."

Old brakes grabbed and slipped as Josh's farm truck came to a half stop. Cranking the steering wheel hard, the truck swayed into a U-turn. Passenger bodies in the back fought for a hand hold.

"There they go, there they go," announced Buck, pointing in the direction of the fading tail lights.

"I know, I know, I am turning," said Josh loudly. "Now get your finger out of my face Buck. I can not drive with it stuck up my nose."

Buck grinned with satisfaction. The shotgun resting between his legs wobbled wildly as the anxiousness of the chase became arousing. Jock and Josh questioned Buck's strange laugh with a side glance of their eyes. Clinging to their every move the second truck squealed into a U-turn, tight onto the bumper of the first.

Spitting chewed portions of the cigar onto the jeep's floor, Reese counted the headlights passing in rapid succession. Reese grabbed at the steering wheel trying to force it free from Fred's hands.

"That is them, turn, turn faster. They are not going to get away from us this time." Reese shoved the cigar deeper into his mouth.

Driving the jeep into the dry ditch, Fred made the turn-around on the softness of a farmer's field before taking back to the highway. Puff dry cattails exploded against the grill of the jeep. Moths and beetles splattered against the windshield leaving a sticky imprint.

"Get this heap onto the highway."

"Next time, leave your hands off the steering wheel," replied Fred, his voice as impatient as that of Reese's.

At seventy miles an hour, Suzie turned her head in the direction of the following headlights. Light brown hair scattered in the wind. Facing forewords, she grabbed at the edge of the seat

"Hang on. We are going to go a little faster," Boo added as he changed gears and pressed the gas pedal.

Pulling up to the side of the truck, Boo held the M.G. steady as he yelled over to Salami. "There are two farmer's trucks, a Jeep and several Bikers tagging along behind us."

"Let's not stay around for the party," suggested Salami. "Split up and try to loose them." Salami waved as he pulled away from Boo, Suzie and the M.G.

CHAPTER 9
FIREWORKS

A parade of unlikely persons and vehicles displayed their talents, though strangely different. If the night wanted to rest, it would be hard to obtain. A bright moon reflected the last of the sun's rays onto the highway running through the grass lands of Alberta. A parade of vehicles sped along the hard top, casting erratic beams of light. Horns blared, voices strained to be heard above the roaring of car engines, and voices of others vying for the same air space.

Jostling for position, as if in a race, two outdated half-ton trucks pushed and shoved a lone battered Jeep along the highway. For whatever reason, each wanted to be the first to advance to the head of the line. Ahead of the assailants where Salami and Tina, followed by Boo and Suzie in the little red car. Zig-zagging like a fly among spiders, the M.G. looked for an exit.

With the swaying of the truck, Tina felt the alcohol doing its best to crawl back up her throat. Swallowing and holding a tight grip to her seat, Tina watched her beloved car from the side mirror. Suzie was having a great time speeding along the highway in the warm breeze, letting her hair blow freely.

Suzie asked above the night sounds of vehicles and voices, "Why are those trucks following us? I know why the bikers are. Henry was kind of cute."

"Henry?"

"We did not do anything to those people in the trucks. Are they after you?"

"Yeah, I kind of know those farmers," Boo replied, changing gears as he spoke. "They are mad at me for spoiling their shotgun wedding." Boo seemed calm about the facts.

Suzie asked anxiously, craving for details, "A wedding, who was it for?"

"A farmer's daughter." Boo was reminded of Irene's warmth and innocence. "Irene."

Suzie's curiosity grew as she pestered for information. "Who was the guy that had to marry the girl?"

"Ahh . . ., me," said Boo, dragging out the words.

"You!" exclaimed Suzie, turning to look back towards the rough condition of the following trucks. "You, if they catch you, I think they are going to string you up for desertion."

Boo smiled at Suzie with self assurance, as he clutched and changed gears. "They have to catch me first, yes they do."

Staring wide eyed for several moments, Suzie was trying to draw some logic from Boo's expression. Boo weaved the M.G. across the highway's centre line.

"This is getting a little dangerous," Tina nervously said to Salami. "Do you think we can get away from whoever is following us?"

"Sure," Salami replied with confidence. "As soon as I find a side road, we will loose them."

"I hope so," sounded Tina's upset voice. "I have more bad news for you."

"More, I do not need more. I think we have had enough to last us for awhile."

"Those . . .,"

"Spit it out. A little more bad news can't hurt us. Will it?" Salami's eyes peered deep into Tina's glazed eyes.

"Okay," Tina shook her head, closed her eyes as she began to say as simply as possible. "Those two men in the grey Jeep, well one is my uncle and the big one, is my Dad."

Tina kept her head down, and eyes closed, while she waited for Salami to say something. Taking awhile for the words to sink into his thick head, Salami pondered the facts before he was able to figure it out.

"Your Dad!" said Salami coldly. "The other guy is your uncle. And Suzie is?"

Tina opened her eyes to look at Salami. "My cousin, and my uncles Daughter."

"Holly shit, Boo!" yelled Salami. Pressing down his foot, the truck began to gain speed. "Reese's daughter. Shit sure happens to Boo."

With truck horns blaring, Salami's attempts to gain Boo's attention was lost in the night filled sounds. Far ahead was the M.G., creating a fair distance from the rest. Salami was pulling away from one of the farmer's trucks with the grey Jeep and another farmer's truck behind. Keeping a safe distance, the bikers were still close enough to be considered in the game of catch them if you can.

"Reese!" yelled out Fred, above the Jeep's rattling. "I think that, the red car is the same as my daughter's?"

"So, it looks the same." Tobacco juice continuously dripped from the edge of Reese's mouth as the excitement of the chase grew.

"The driver resembles that Boo fellow." Fred's big hands twisted around the large steering wheel. "It is your daughter sitting in the passenger seat!"

Reese attempted to spit, only to have the juice drip down his chin. "That is the car we follow. Fred, do not loose them."

Fred changed gears, forcing the Jeep to jump forward, its metal twisting under the strain. Thoughts of what to do were scrambled in the heads of both men. Things were becoming complicated. Their daughters were involved. Maybe that was a good excuse to justify their intent to harm Boo and Salami.

Reese's words were lost beneath the sound of the Jeep's engine. "I will make sure Boo crawls and begs for mercy when I get through with him.

Fred cocked an ear, wondering if he had heard Reese. Then again, Fred would be applying pain to anyone that hurt his daughter. 'Where is my daughter?' questioned Fred of his thoughts.

Sleeping streets of Medicine Hat became a play ground of mazes. Off the main street, Boo and Salami turned their vehicles onto side streets, attempt to lose their followers. Roaring bikes, a Jeep and trucks awoke the town with their squealing tires and stammering engines. Salami turned onto a parallel street, heading directly west out of town.

Boo began to like the way the little red car handled. Tight turns and instant speed on the short streets was a boost to their getaway. Holding onto the seat, Suzie closed eyes each time the car slid around a corner. Turned off lights would help keep the car from being easily noticed. High whining of the car's engine echoed unmistakably through the streets of Medicine Hat.

"Look out!" yelled Tina, grabbing at Salami's arm. "Look . . .!"

Pulling hard on the steering wheel left through the intersection, Salami faced the oncoming Jeep. Fred swerved off to the right, avoiding a collision. Hitting a row of garbage cans lining the side of the street sounded like a perfect strike in a bowling alley.

"Get back onto the road," hollered Reese, his face a repulsive smirk. From his lap, Reese tossed a slimy packet of garbage that felt mushy between his fingers.

Fred hollered back, "I am trying."

Though trying, the Jeep headed onto the sidewalk hitting another row of garbage cans with repeated accuracy. Metal bent and twisted under the Jeep's tires. Fred wheeled the Jeep onto the street.

"Do not gab my arm like that," Salami managed to say after turning another corner. "We could have hit those jerks."

Feeling a little insulted by Salami's remarks, Tina retorted, "Do not say that. One of those jerks is my father."

"At least you agree."

Salami began to laugh out loud. Soon afterwards, Tina began to build into laughter as she realized the irony of the situation. She was now actually beginning to enjoy the thrill of the chase.

"Take a right, right here," demanded Tina with authority in her voice.

"Okay Boss!" Salami cranked the tires right. The light back end of the truck bounced several times into a straight direction.

Stopped at a red light, Josh and Jock were arguing with Buck about which direction the red car had last gone. Each convinced that the direction they were pointing in was the right one. Under the glow of street lights, a blur of red passed in-front of the farmer's truck. Only Buck seemed to notice the incident.

Jock pointed straight ahead. "I am sure they went straight up this street."

"They are heading east, behind us," Josh's voice was several notches above his usual low talk of a pleasant farmer.

With a hand gripping the barrel of the shotgun, Buck began to grin with excitement. Bouncing with childishness, Buck pointed in-front of Josh. "You are both wrong, they just went that way." Buck slapped the dash board repetitively until Josh and Jock paid attention.

Weak eyes watched the dark shadow fade down the darkened street.

"Stop, stop!" Suzie covered eyes with a shaking hand.

"Too late," said Boo, pulling the wheels left then right.

Passing through the intersection at the same time, the biker's engines roared, breaking the peacefulness of silence. A whining of a car's engine was mute to the distinctive signature of the Harley Davidson's. Boo managed not to collide with the bikers as he squirmed between the bikes and the trike.

Speed slammed a foot onto the brake leaver bring the trike to a stop in the middle of the intersection. Heads followed the escaping red M.G.. A sudden blare of horns sent shivers up the spines of the trio sitting on the trike. Echoing horns were too close for comfort. Speed turned to face the oncoming head-lights of the farmer's trucks. With instant fright, Snow and Coke clasped arms around Speed's head. One truck passed behind, the other in-front. Yelling, firearm toting farmers hollered from the backs of the trucks. not until the sounds had faded into the distance did Speed attempt to look about.

"Let go of my head, you dumb broads." Speed wrestled free of the girl's hold. "What the hell you broads trying to do, yank my head off."

Hooker and the other two bikers turned at the sound of the horns. Passing by Speed, who tried to escape the clutches of the girls, the others followed the fading sounds of the horns.

"Get back in your seats you dumb broads!" yelled Speed, cranking the trike into a wheelie, and squealing from the intersection.

Passing in opposite directions, the red M.G., and the porcupine truck passed by each other. Arms and hands waved hellos and goodbyes. Tina seemed to be indulging in the excitement of the moment, as she egged Salami on. Salami followed orders, giving the truck a burst of speed.

"That is my daughter's car!" shouted Fred, after seeing the small car pass. "I am going after it."

Without disagreement, Reese held on for the ride. Hands held fast to the body of the Jeep as it wobbled into a U-turn. Blinding light hit them dead on from approaching vehicles. Screeching tires resisted the meshing of rubber and asphalt as the farmer's trucks came to a rattling stop. Kinfolk in the back of the trucks bounced together like marbles in a washing machine.

Hearts stopped beating as a loud crack echoed above all other sounds. Shotgun bee-bees from a discharged gun sent the street light into darkness. Tinkling glass dropped to the pavement in a shower of little sparkling coloured lights. Kinfolk looked about each other with questioning eyes, as they were tossed about by the wobbling trucks.

"What in tar-nation was that?" yelled Josh out through the window. Putting the truck into gear, Josh began to follow the maroon truck.

Undecided, as to which vehicle to purse, or in which direction to head, the bikers circled their bikes around the intersection. Like circus bears trained to ride on motor bikes, the bikers performed for the growing spectators looking down from apartment windows.

A city once asleep, awoke to what might have sounded like the Indy 500. Trucks, bikes, a car and a Jeep, raced up and down most streets of the sleeping town. Horns blaring, tires squealing, voices echoing through the empty streets greeted the early morning hours that showed the time on the city's clock.

Up and down and across the many streets of town raced this carnival of people. The prey searching for an exit out of town to safety, the hunters seeking out their evasive prey.

Warm air streamed above the ground. Thinking that they had eluded their followers, Boo and Suzie headed towards the outskirts of Medicine Hat. Boo was enjoying the fast pace of the night. Riding around in the little M.G. made him feel like a kid. From the smiles, frowns and the display of facial expressions on her face, Suzie reluctantly enjoyed her first night in this small prairie town.

"My Dad is going to kill me," Suzie said, after pondering the joys of the chase. "He knows it was me, I just know it. And I am with a strange man."

Would Boo make the connection, would he realize that one of his pursuers, Reese, was Suzie's father?

"I am not strange," protested Boo. "If you are scared of life. Scared of living what life has to offer, then go back to Mommy and Daddy. You can watch life pass you by from the comfort of your bedroom."

"When my Dad gets his hands on me, I will be locked in my room for eternity."

Slowing the M.G. to a stop on the soft shoulder, Boo waited for Suzie to give an indication of what she planed to do.

Stepping from the car, Suzie walked aimlessly around with a bowed head cradled in agitated fingers. Keeping her head bent forward left thoughts, of her life style, her parents and her wants, juggling themselves in her mind. Had her parents been over protective and controlling? Longing for moments of freedom like this, where she could let go of her inhibitions, was a taste of the wilder side of life she wanted to explore. Suzie's mind was made up. Now to follow through on her thoughts.

"Okay, I will," She said, getting back into the car. Wiping the corner of her eyes with her palms, Suzie brushed back lightly tangled hair. "I would like to see what is down the road." An excited nervousness jiggled in her stomach.

Boo gave her a smile, as he put the little car into movement. Suzie lifted her head. Eyes, of deep blue, seemed to return a smile.

"Okay, let's move'em out," Boo attempted to say in a John Wayne drawl.

"That was terrible."

"Critics everywhere."

A night made for lovers to be strolling through a park, this would be the ideal night. Life is never like the movies. Boo and Suzie were together, so to say, but far from strolling through a park. The night was the only setting left. Making the best of the night was to find a hiding place safe from the farmers and rejected bikers.

Regardless of the severity of the situation, Salami's mind was always on the one he was with. Providing that his passenger was a female. Even though Tina was beginning to enjoy the excitement of the chase, she did not welcome Salami's advances. Being cute and somewhat amusing to be with, Tina did not want to advance into a romantic affair with Salami. This was her summer to have fun before entering college. Fun was to be spent with Suzie. Tina wondered if Suzie was having merriment.

"Keep your hands on the steering wheel." Tina pulled Salami's hand from her shoulder. She did not let go of it completely. "Keep your thoughts on driving this truck safely."

"Why, you are more arousing to handle than this truck?" Salami's hand explored Tina's neck.

Was it the after feeling of alcohol, the advances by Salami, or her own need to share in the high of the moment. Tina wanted to play. Reaching along Salami's arm, Tina rubbed her hand over his chest. To her surprise, she enjoyed the firmness when his chest rose with each breath.

"We may have to do something about your arousal," purred Tina's voice.

Looking in the rear-view mirror, and both of the truck's side mirrors, Salami surveyed the rear for any signs of headlights following. To his pleasure, the night was dark and void of any pursuers.

"And what did you have in mind?" Salami sounded a little too anxious as he attempted to kiss Tina about the neck. From lack of attendance, the truck swerved from side to side. Tina fought off Salami's advances, just slightly.

"Pull off the road someplace, and let's see what develops." Tina's eyes sent vibrating temptations surging through Salami's mind.

Smiling coolly, trying not to show too much enthusiasm, Salami made a move. Words of an invitation had left Tina's lips. Too late to be recalled. Salami turned sharply to the right. Loose gravel rattled in the wheel wells of the truck. Pot holes lined the seldom used lane-way which intersected sections of pasture land. There seemed to be no end, or destination of the pathway.

Too occupied with bracing themselves, when the truck bounced and swayed, Salami and Tina paid no attention to the eeriness within the darkness. The lane-way turned from a path-way to a pair of wheel ruts creased into the hard dry earth. Salami tried once to look in the mirror for any sings of followers. There was nothing behind them. In the back of Salami's mind was Tina's invitation. In the front of his mind was his ability to concentrate on driving.

Brush, weeds, and tall grass lined the path of travel. Vast, even haunting seemed the marsh land that banked the sides of the path. A slight haze hovered a foot above the slimy water. The scene was ideal for a vampire movie. Anything could be hiding, ready to pounce upon prey. Expecting the unexpected usually happens.

Seeing that further travel was becoming difficult, Salami stopped the truck, turning off the headlights. Darkness made Tina unconsciously move closer to Salami's side. With a kiss to Tina's neck, Salami was back to the invitation. Beyond the confines of the truck, the sounds of croaking frogs, crickets and a hoot from an Owl in the distance echoed natures sounds of mating.

After crawling through the window between the cab and the cap, the mating sounds of humans filtered out to the outside world. The basics of need is natural in nature.

Suzie looked back, looking for any signs of someone following them. Seeing nothing, she was relieved, but still unsure of herself and where she was. After all, Boo was a complete stranger. Maybe, sometimes, it is easier to be yourself when one is with a stranger.

"We can not drive forever," announced Boo, claiming Suzie's attention. "I think we should stop and wait until morning before we continue."

"Stop where?" Suzie replied. "Where are we going to stop out here?"

"Anywhere out of sight of those bikers, farmers and those two old guys in an old army Jeep." Boo looked over anticipating a quick remark.

For someone running with a nice looking young woman, Boo was finding it hard to get to first base with her. Boo wondered if Salami was running into the same problem with Tina. It is the nature of the beast that man seeks the pleasure of a woman under any circumstance. One would not be human unless the animal instincts stirred the hormones. Salami's ways were crude at times, though he did alright with the girls.

Boo glanced at Suzie, she held her thoughts and words to herself. 'Well,' Boo thought to himself. 'We are going to stop no matter what she thinks or says.'

At a random place, Boo drove the red car off the road through a low graded ditch onto a freshly cut field. Keeping his foot on the accelerator, the car fish-tailed across the field.

"What are you doing?" A surprised frown reflected from her face under the glow of the dashboard lights. "Are you some kind of nut?"

Boo thought over the question. With a devilish smile, Boo answered, "I guess so. It is the only way to be."

In the open field, there was not too many places to hide. Staying out in the open, someone was bound to see the small car. The only cover was between two hay stacks standing perfectly coned in the centre of the field. Boo stared for a moment at Suzie's breasts rising with each breath. The similarities between them and the hay stacks were only in Boo's thoughts. Racing at full throttle, Boo aimed the car towards the cleavage of the two hay stacks. Suzie placed both hands over her eyes, refusing to witness the outcome of Boo's actions.

It was a tight squeeze. Loose hay billowed then came to rest on and around the car. Slamming the brakes on at the right moment left the car concealed from a distant view. A flip of a switch popped the convertible top. Clasping the top to the windshield, loose hay rested on the top like sprinkles of snow.

Boo drew in a breath of aroma. Drying hay sweat to the nasal senses.

"It smells like shit," Suzie's point of view. "You are nuts."

"Thank you." Boo beamed a big smile. "At lest we are hidden."

Suzie brushed strands of hay from her lap. Folding arms across a heaving chest, she covered Boo's intended view. At the moment, Boo decided to pass on making a pass. Suzie's turned away head was a strong deterrent.

Making himself comfortable in the reclined seat, Boo welcomed a simple rest. "Goodnight Miss," he said politely.

Beneath the insulated hay the dampness of the ground was kept a bay. Crickets sung a lullaby to the dreamless sleepers.

Rays of the sun's warmth heated the blacktop of the Alberta highway. Mist rose from the damp fields as morning began to wake. Eyes strained to scan the distances. Farmers lined the north side of the highway with shotguns cradled in their arms. In an open Jeep, Fred and Reese fought off the morning dampness from the south side of the highway. From east and west the roar of motorcycles disturbed the morning's tranquility. Parking some thirty feet from the farmers, the bikers idled their bikes, as they pondered their next move.

For the most part of the early hours, the three groups of predators staked out a section of the secondary highway. Vultures perched waiting for their next meal. Sitting astride of their bikes, the bikers let their idling engines disturb the patience of the others. With a shotgun butt wedged under an arm pit, Josh strolled towards the bikers.

"Any more noise from those machines," spoke Josh, in a pleasant voice above the irritating sound. "and they will be leaking oil and air." Josh raised the barrel level with the gas tank of Hooker's bike.

Fearless of intimidation, Hooker hesitated. Wanting to say something, Hooker changed his mind when Josh took another step forward. One after another, a biker cut his engine, following Hooker's example.

This small incident seemed to be the only incident of the morning. All were waiting for a truck, or a little red car to appear out of nowhere. Neither Boo or Salami wished to make an entrance into the hands of their pursuers.

Covered under a sleeping bag, Salami and Tina rolled about unwilling to let the night end. There was no need to depart, no need to venture outside of their playground. Mist hovered and shielded the truck until the full heat of the morning burnt off the moisture. No need to hurry away. Tina and Salami's play, postponed departure indefinitely.

Not waiting for Suzie to wake, Boo started the car. Under full acceleration, the car pushed its way out from under the loose hay of the twin hay stacks. Clinging stems of hay dispersed in the air as the car made its way across the field. A trail of hay showed the direction of the departing car.

Boo said good morning to the only other passenger awake this morning. On the dash, licking its paws, sat a small white field mouse. Looking up when Boo spoke, it returned to its morning cleansing ritual. Boo tossed hay from the Red M.G. as it crawled back onto the highway. Driving down the highway expecting the farmers, bikers and Jeep to pounce on him, Boo was glad to see the highway empty in both directions. Suzie slept with her head resting on praying hands. Even the little mouse was curled up on a nest of hay. Rays of sun through the windshield warmed its tiny body.

Pulling into the first rest stop he saw, Boo left his passengers to sleep. Needed food and a release of the bladder were of necessity. Making eye contact with an middle aged waitress, Boo ordered a double bacon sandwich before heading to the facilities.

Sitting down at the counter, Boo eyed the current surroundings. To his right sat a trucker, a big dude. An elderly couple in their seventies sat to Boo's left at the end of the white counter. Besides the waitress, was the short order cook behind the half wall. Boo smiled with friendliness when eye contact was made.

Waking with a start, Suzie viewed the unfamiliar surroundings. Seeing the hay, see recalled the past night's dilemma. Removing the hay clinging to her, Suzie startled the sleeping mouse which in turn startled her. Shrieking, Suzie jumped from the seat to the parking lot slamming the door behind her. Holding her hands to ears until calming down, Suzie pranced with the need to pee.

Storming through the Dinner, Suzie headed directly to the washrooms. From the look on her face everyone in the room knew that Suzie was not a morning person. Grumpy, miserable, discontented, yes, all the above.

Boo was in the middle of a bite full of the bacon sandwich when Suzie sat down on a wobbling stool beside him. "Good morning. Did you sleep well?"

"Never mind how I slept," grouchy was her tone. "What are you eating?"

"Food. Do you know what food is?" answered and asked sarcastically by Boo.

"Funny, very funny."

"Would you care for something to eat?"

The waitress took Suzie's order, as she cut a piece of Boston Cream pie for the elderly woman. A smile glanced towards Boo faded when the waitress looked back at Suzie. 'A slight touch of jealousy,' thought Boo, smiling to himself.

Finishing the sandwich, Boo downed it with orange juice as Suzie started to ask questions.

"Where are we, and where are you taking me?"

Leaning with a turned head, the truck driver had a concerned eye cast in Boo's direction.

"I do not know, and we are going that way." Boo pointed west.

White haired old folks looked out of the Dinner's window expecting to see something.

"What about Tina and your friend Salami?" It was obvious that Suzie's temper was beginning to flare.

"I do not know where they are. I bet they are having a better time then we are."

"Well, you are not much fun to be with either," yelled Suzie, so that all could hear. "I was dumped with you. It was not my idea to go with you in the first place."

From behind the half wall, the cook poked his head out to see what the raised voices were all about.

"Then take your ass outside and hitch a ride back to where you came from." Boo turned to face the dead pan look on the truck driver's face. "She . . ., escaped from an institution."

Suzie's eyes flared angrily. Steam was building under her collar. Reaching across the counter, she picked up the Boston Cream pie. Turning back just in time to see the pie in the air, Boo ducked out of the way. Splat, then the clank of the tin pie plate against the counter top sounded. Suzie's hand covered her gaping mouth, her eyes expressed amazement. Looking in the direction of the throw, Boo watched the cream pie sag slowly from the trucker's face. Two huge fingers scraped the cream from his eyes. Black eyes beneath the yellow cream and white toping stared directly at Boo.

Boo cocked a thumb back towards Suzie. "Had I mentioned the institution?"

Shaking the cream from his hands, the trucker reached over the counter. Chocolate cream pie topped with whipped cream rested in his huge hand. Boo and Suzie leaned sideways as the pie sailed through the air.

"Eek...!" screamed the waitress. "Look out!" She backed away from the counter. The cook's eyes peeked over the lip of the wall.

Splat sounded the direct hit. Cream splashed in all directions. Like a bowling pin teetering before it falls, the elderly woman rocked to and fro on the stool. Licking the cream from her lips, she turned to her husband for sympathy. The big trucker was motionless as he watched the old man stand to his feet. No expression could be seen on the old man's face. Straightening spectacles, he took a cane in hand and walked towards the huge trucker.

Bushy hair and thick eyebrows peered directly into the old fellow's beady eyes. Before the trucker was able to react, the old man crowned him once, twice, three times before backing away. Floundering, the trucker backed up trying to stay on small feet. Tables and chairs interrupted his fall as he crashed to the checkerboard tiled floor.

With the commotion taking place, Boo decided it was a good time to leave. Cleaning out a pocket, Boo placed a fist full of bills on the counter. One hand grabbed Suzie by the shoulder, the other clutched her order of turkey on whole wheat. Before she realized it, Suzie was being stuffed into the little red M.G..

"Remind me not to take you anywhere."

"That mouse has to go or I do."

"That mouse would probably be better company than you," replied Boo, starting the car's engine. "You are welcome to get out and stay here."

"Okay I am going with you," pouted Suzie, her eyes staring at the white mouse curled up in its nest.

"And that mouse stays."

To Boo's comfort, the traffic heading northward was beginning to become congested. There is a safety in numbers. Being lost in the crowd was a good place to be. Still, Boo kept a wandering eye looking out for the farmers, bikers and Reese. Comfort would be ditching Suzie and this car, finding Salami and his truck, then getting out of town.

Walking into a Dinner that seemed like it was hit by an earthquake, Salami and Tina were afraid to ask questions.

"We are closed until I get this mess cleaned up," informed a waitress, down on hands and knees.

"A major food fight?" asked Salami, as he began to identify the different messes. "Apple pie, Chilly, Boston and Chocolate cream pies."

"What happened here?" asked Tina, concerned about the work the waitress was going through.

"A nice-looking guy, driving a fancy red car came in. A nice guy. Then some strange girl started it, she threw a pie. My regular customers ended up fighting, a seventy nine year old couple fighting with a trucker." sighed the waitress, moving cream into a gooey pile. "That old man belted the trucker with his cane. I am a nervous wreck." Standing, she wiped her forehead with a cream filled towel. She pointed strangely towards Tina. "That girl looked like you."

"Boo and Suzie," announced Salami and Tina simultaneously.

"How long ago? Did you see which direction they were headed?"

Fatigue was drained from the waitress, she seemed ready to collapse. "The car headed north about two hours ago." She said, walking towards the kitchen.

Doing without a meal, Salami and Tina headed in a northerly direction. It was their hope to meet up with Boo and Suzie before anyone else did. Searching was one thing, finding them was another matter. Obviously, Boo and Suzie would be searching for Salami and Tina. Somewhere on the many back roads, or through small prairie towns, they were bound to find each other.

Tired and stiff from lack of sleep and movement, the bikers, farmers, Reese and Fred waited by the side of the secondary highway. All waited with anticipation that Boo or Salami would drive by. Looking up and down the highway, then looking at each other, they waited for the other to make the first move. Maybe the other knew something, or had an idea.

Reese glanced at his watch through blurred eyes. Noting the time, Reese spoke to Fred. "It is after one o'clock. Maybe they left the area last night." Reese scratched static eyebrows. "Start the Jeep."

As soon as the sound of the engine fired to a start, the bikers straddled their bikes. Josh motioned to his other kin to pile into the trucks.

"Which way Reese?" Fred waited for an answer.

"That way, you fool." Reese pointed west. A cigar used beyond its worth was cast to the ground. From a chest pocket, Reese retrieved a fresh stubby.

As soon as the Jeep took to the highway, the farmers pulled out right behind them. The familiar clatter of bike engines lagged in a position behind the farm trucks.

"Do they know where they are going Josh?" inquisitively asked Jock.

"I am not sure. It will not be a disadvantage if we follow."

As eager as the first taste of the chase, Buck's face showed a sickly grin of enjoyment. Yellowish hair spiked on his head suited his diluted intelligence.

Speed pulled up beside Hooker. Yelling above the roar of engines he said. "The girls say they are hungry." Snow and Coke nodded their heads.

"Too dam bad." Hooker turned with a deviant smile. "When we get our hands on those young tight-ass`es, Snow and Coke can cut the guys up for a meal."

Speed gritted teeth in a satisfied manner. Showing their disapproval, the girls gave Hooker upturned fingers.

No-one passed or attempted to pass the parade of fools. Every group kept their position while the afternoon dwindled. The towns of Redcliff, Suffield and Alderson were passed through as the parade approached the town of Brooks.

Brooks, a sleepy town where people pass and later forget. A town not worth remembering. Nothing out of the ordinary happened in this sleepy town over the past fifty years. Families have come and gone with few things changing in the town's way of life. There is still an odd person or two that could remember back fifty years.

In this town, about a mile from the town's only paved street, lives a person that able to remember back fifty years. As a matter of fact, he can remember back eighty-nine years, give or take the first few years as a baby.

To most folks living near by, he was the best of a neighbor. That was up until his wife passed away a year or so back. Now he keeps to himself, seldom seeing anyone for weeks on end. Kids that once visited the old man on his farm were shooed away. Sometimes they were chased away with rock-salt fired from a single shot shotgun. Curiosity would not keep the kids away when they were trying to see what the old man was up to.

A once flourishing farm, now housed the odd cows, pigs and chickens. The old red barn that once held fifty milk cows was now locked up and it's windows covered.

Stories flowed. Rumors were that the old man was crazy or drunk most of the time. So crazy, the stories say, that he was going to blow up the barn. Kids hiding in the tall grass swore they saw the old man put hundreds of explosives inside the barn. Boxes after boxes were carried into the barn. Each box had red letters saying, 'Danger, Explosives.'

They were just stories, parents would tell each other. Were they just stories? Only old man Perkins would know, but no-one ever asked him. Then again no-one could ever get close enough to his place to ask.

Night after night on the porch sat a white haired shell of a man. Happy smiles that people remembered were gone from his face, gone forever. Sitting in a rocking chair, sipping whisky, he sat guarding the barn with a rock-salt filled shotgun. So the kids would say. Night after night he and an old hound dog, as old as old man Perkins, watched from the lantern lite porch.

Far westward, tower the snow capped Rocky Mountains. Huge and massive, they loom as if floating on the rolling sea of foot hills along the Alberta boarder. Standing there facing those monoliths, one feels if an arm was to be stretched out, a hand would be able to touch the jagged rocks. While the sun climbed over the shapely peeks, shadows changed and danced in a kaleidoscope of changing scenes.

Facing the afternoon show, one of the last drive-in fast food outlets hosted locals and tourists heading towards the majestic mountains. Hunger pains had enticed Reese and Fred to pull into the burger joint. Sheep following their leader entered the parking spaces under the canopy. Taking a spot in the middle, Reese and Fred faced the farmers across the centre walkway. Keeping a distance, the bikers congregated at the end with their backs against the panoramic view of wonder.

Interest in the scenery was not what they were here for. While tourists clicked away with cameras from small to large, the parade of followers watched each other. Every move, every facial expression was questioned. Why was the other after Boo and Salami? Who the hell were Boo and Salami, that would have these men tracking them. Unlike the bikers, that did not seem to have a purpose in life, Josh had a farm to run. Likely, his kin had farm chores piling up back home. Reese was enjoying a vacation with a sinister motive.

All were waiting. Someone was bound to make a move. One among them would make a decision. It seemed obvious that not one of them had any idea where Boo and Salami were. There were no clues as to where they could be. The fact that the two boys had split up, diminished the chances of catching even one of the two.

Josh leaned over the steering wheel, peering directly into Reese's eyes. Cold eyes reflected cold eyes. Hooker and the bikers where on the chase to satisfy the need to live up to their image. An image Henry assumed, a need to be close to his brother. Some people are meant to be followers, people that hang on, go with the flow. Going with the flow is not always the best for an individual. It is easier to follow than stand on one's own two feet. A finger of blame is equally pointed at the leader and those that follow.

Fred, Buck, Hog and the others willingly follow regardless of the penalties that may befall upon them due to the actions of their leaders. Without followers, there may not be leaders. Whether for good or bad, the system of leaders and followers works.

Taking the last mouthful of a greasy hamburger, Reese stuffed a chewed cigar into his mouth. Swallowing and puffing seemed to go unnoticed by Reese, who at this point in time had only Boo's capture on his mind. Tossing the last of a burger to the ground, Reese motioned to Fred to start the Jeep. It was time to do something. Somehow, find a lead, a clue. Reese was going to be the leader.

No sooner had the Jeep's engine started when the others followed suit. Again the parade headed onto the highways in search of Salami and Boo. Eyes of peaceful residents in Brooks watched the strangeness of the searches crawling up and down the streets of their sleepy little town.

Knowing that it was Tuesday, about ten boys and girls, ranging in ages from eight to twelve, gathered at the edge of the path leading to old man Perkins' barn. All knew that after supper a delivery truck would bring several boxes to old man Perkins' place. Every week the boxes would arrive. This had been going on for almost a month and a half. Boxes a foot and a half square. What caught the eyes of the kids were the words printed on the sides of the wooden crates, 'DANGER EXPLOSIVES'.

Old man Perkins knew that the kids were hiding in the tall grass by the path. As long as they did not come too close to the barn, he would not have to chase them away. The shotgun filled with rock-salt was just an incentive to keep kids away. He liked kids. Well that was what he mentioned to the delivery guy. It was just that right now, he just could not have kids hanging around. Nodding several times in reply, the delivery guy unloaded the boxes and left.

Big creaking barn doors swung open when old man Perkins leaned on them with all the strength his old body could muster. One by one he placed the boxes to the side as he shooed away some chickens. Leaving the red barn doors open while he went to a smaller side building, the kids had a clear view of what was stored. From behind tall grass, the kids strained their eyes from heads stretched to the maximum. Hoping that old man Perkins would forget about the open doors and head into the house, the kids waited with eager anticipation. Only the bravest kid would attempt to enter the barn then report back. Across the dusty driveway towards the house, old man Perkins chased an old rooster. Big red barn doors stayed open. Kid's eyes widened.

Cresting a small grade, Boo could See his truck a mile ahead. Clutching, Boo put the M.G. into top gear. The sudden jerk of the car awoke the sleeping mouse. Speed closed the distance between the two vehicles. A constant beep of the car's horn gained Salami's attention. Seeing nothing ahead, Boo pulled the car into the opposite lane in an attempt to pull along side of the maroon truck.

As the curve in the highway straightened out, a parade of fools were seen approaching in the distance. Reese and Fred in their Jeep led, with Josh and kin following. Holding a close distance behind were Hooker and the other bikers.

At the same instant the searchers were spotted, Boo and Salami cut the wheels of their vehicles to the right. Dust billowed from the dirt road that they took to escape. Suzie held a hand over her mouth to block the dust. On the dash the small white mouse crawled under its bundle of hay. No-one noticed the sign at the head of the road saying, 'The Perkins Place'.

More excited than ever was Buck, as he bounced in the seat. Hands griping the shotgun barrel, stroked up and down with each bump of the truck. Josh and Jock resembled frowning book ends on either side of Buck.

Fred's large frame held its place on the small seat. With hands gripped across the dash, Reese chomped feverishly on the shredded cigar. Chocking dust hid the view ahead of them.

Lagging far in the rear, the bikers on their street machines crawled over and around the road's irregularities. Black leather suits turned a dull grey under the clinging dust.

Tiring of the bumps and dust, Boo headed right into a field of tall hay. Salami bounced overturned sod leading into the open field to his left. Splitting up, the followers picked a prey to follow. A Jeep and two bikers, Hooker and Henry followed Boo and Suzie. Following the cut of the field was easy on the little car. Cutting across the field, the jeep bounced heavily, slowing down their speed. Tall hay obscured the biker's view. Roaring bikes made trails that lead nowhere but into endless circles.

Salami and Tina laughed together, as if this was a joyful amusement ride. Hog and Speed were totally lost in the endless tall hay. At every bump of uneven ground, the old farmer's trucks would bounce and shake the life out of their frames. Kinfolk hanging on in the open back bounced out of the box into the sea of tall grass. Soon a trail of farmers lined the path cleared by the truck. Josh slowed down enough to let his lost cargo catch a ride at a run.

"That was an easy getaway," said Suzie, when they came to a road at the end of the field. "I think we have lost them for the moment."

Boo glanced back to confirm. Suzie looked a bit scared. Her hands held tightly to the seat as the car raced down the road leading left. Only for a second did the mouse stick out its head to see the outcome of the ride. Not being satisfied that the ride was over, back under the hay it stuck its head. Suzie seemed to have no choice other than to enjoy the ride.

Billowing dust moving towards each other followed Boo and Salami. On the single lane road, friends were on a collision course. At the last second, Boo turned onto a driveway. Salami quickly followed as the trailing dust storms swallowed each other.

"That was close," yelled Tina, bouncing from side to side for just the pleasure of it. "A natural rush."

"There will probably be more to come," added Salami, his voice showing a childish excitement at having the first ride down the big kid's playground slide.

Rusting, forgotten farm equipment lined the roadway leading into the open area in front of a farm yard. There seemed to be no exit from the yard. Boo slammed on the brakes of the car. Old age seemed to have taken over the once luster of the red M.G.. Unable to stop as suddenly, Salami swerved around the car. Passing through the barn doors, the truck came to a stop inside of the barn. Thinking that it was a good hiding place, Boo followed into the darkness of the big red faded barn.

From their hiding place in the tall grass, the kids watched the happenings without uttering a word. Eyes widened, mouths fell open. Old man Perkins stuck his head out of an upstairs window when he heard the sounds of vehicles out side. All that his old eyes saw was the dissipating dust storm at the end of his driveway. Slowly he went about house cleaning. Several times he adjusted a hanging picture of his wife before becoming satisfied. Old man Perkins smiled.

Tina and Salami jumped from the truck, little kids having the fun of their lives. Boo bounced over the closed car door to greet his friend. Suzie stayed in seat. White knuckles remained fastened over the front of the leather seat.

"How are you doing man?" said Boo, sticking out a hand to receive a slap in gesture of hello.

"Great Boo," a smile on Salami's face confirmed it. "Could not be better." Salami's eyes pointed to a giggling Tina.

"You do not seem to be having as much fun as Salami and I," Tina said, looking over to Suzie sitting in the car.

"She ain't no bowl of cherries," announced Boo.

"I will have a talk with her, okay?" suggested Tina. "Maybe I can change her mind about you."

Boo nodded as Tina walked towards the red M.G.. Salami and Boo looked around the barn. Their eyes were adjusting to the dim filtered light. A warm dry smell of old hay and dung lingered in the air.

"Any suggestions on what we are going to do Salami?"

"Not a one." Salami shook his head of blonde hair, as if there was not a thought in his mind. "It is not going to take long before those . . ., those people find us."

Salami's eyes wandered through the arched rafters and the vacant stalls to the boxes stacked to the side near old cow yokes.

"A place to hide, we need a place to hide."

Salami was not listening to Boo. Following in the direction of Salami's stare, Boo eyed the same boxes.

"Explosives," uttered Salami in a low soft voice.

"What kind of Explosives. All it says is 'Danger, Explosives'."

"Dy-no-mite," expressed Salami eagerly.

"That should scare them off," said Boo, rubbing hands together, imitating a sinister villain.

Ready made explosives with attached fuses made the art of blasting easy. Light the fuse and throw. Salami removed several butane igniters from a shelf. Handing one to Boo, Salami tested his. A light blue fame popped from the torch tip.

"Nice, it will work just fine." agreed Salami with himself.

With help from the girls, the boys loaded several boxes into the front seat of the truck and car. At that moment, the roar of bikes was heard making their way towards them on the dirt driveway.

"What is that?" ask Suzie.

"Let's go," Salami said to Tina, holding the truck door open for her. "See you later Boo."

"Later," replied Boo, jumping into the driver's seat of the cramped little car.

There was no time to back out through the front doors of the barn. Salami eased the truck's bumper against the back barn doors. With a little pressure the old doors popped from its latch, swinging open to the back pasture. Tires grabbed for traction on the tall grass. As if slipping on patches of black ice, the back ends of the vehicles fish-tailed down the field.

After hearing the gunning of engines mixed with the unmistakable sound of motorcycles, old man Perkins hurried out to the yard. From the flower lined pathway, Perkins watched the bikes enter the barn at full speed. With a limp in his fast walk, old man Perkins leaned a hand against the open barn door and peeked in. Behind the tall grass, the kids had their hands over their ears. Wide eyed kids watched with baited excitement for whatever was about to happen.

Under a billowing cloud of dust and scrambling chickens, a parade of vehicles followed one another into the barn. It was Hog who had noticed the boxes of explosives first. A leather gloved hand smashed the wood slats of a box open. Reaching in, Hog took a hand full of sticks. Following suit, Hooker did the same. Snow grabbed a full box placing it on the trike between herself and Coke.

When their eyes adjusted to the dim light inside of the barn, Fred and Reese along with the farmers observed what the bikers were doing. There was no time to decide what was inside of the boxes. No need to question their own actions. Reese placed several boxes on the floor in front of his seat. The farmers tossed boxes to their kin in the back of the trucks as if they were sacks of potatoes.

Old man Perkins hid behind the barn door, peeking around the corner only when he heard the vehicles advancing out through the barn's back doors. As the dust settled to the ground, old man Perkins entered the barn. Scratching his head behind an ear, Perkins squinted an eye towards the missing boxes of explosives. These sudden past events needed to be pondered. After seventy years of farming, Perkins knew there was no urgency to rush to conclusions. Ambling back towards the house and porch, old man Perkins relaxed his old frame onto an oak rocking chair. A bewildered gaze was cast towards the open doors of the barn. Beyond the barn he observed the fleeing thieves.

Under the creaking sounds of the old rocking chair, the hidden kids, behind the grass bounced their eyes from the field back to old man Perkins.

Boo handed Suzie the small butane torch. With one hand steering, his other hand lifted open the box top.

"And what am I suppose to do with this?" Suzie asked, looking at the little flame thrower. "I do not think that I am having fun yet."

"Try!" Boo gave Suzie a stern gaze. "When I pull out a stick . . .," Boo eyed the funny shaped sticks. ". . ., you take the torch and light the fuse for me."

"Oh, that should be real fun!" Suzie sarcastically answered, testing the torch by pressing the trigger. "Fun for you is blowing up people with dynamite?"

"I am not going to blow people up. We throw the sticks behind us and make holes in the ground." Boo pulled the car out of another fish-tail. "The holes will slow those guys down a bit so that we can escape."

Holding up an odd shaped stick for Suzie, Boo waited for it to be lit. Salami headed towards the left of the field. Boo turned right towards a field lacking growth. The little car rattled when the tires hit the hard pan surface of the field. A familiar sound of bikes were close behind the Red dust caked M.G..

"Look Miss. Virgin, if those bikers get their hands on you, you will not have anything too righteous to write home about." Boo extended an arm, a stick of explosives dangling in front of Suzie's prudish face. "If you do not want their fiendish hands swarming over your body, you had better light this fuse fast."

With a trigger finger faster than thoughts, Suzie sparked the torch at the end of the fuse. Tinny sparks leaped from the fuse as the fire made its way along the length of fiber. Boo waited until he thought the fuse had burnt long enough. A hard backhand toss sent the stick of explosives sailing into the air. Just before it landed on the ground it exploded and fizzled into a cluster of sparks.

Looking back in anticipation of a huge explosion, Suzie smirked. "I think that one was a dud."

A wooden fence topped with barbed wire guarded the end of the field. Beyond the fence stretched a muddy pool of marsh water. Both Boo and Salami reached the fence and turned in a direction heading towards each other. Stopping side by side facing an oncoming attack from their pursuers, Boo and Salami were ready to take on the onslaught. Tina and Suzie sparked their butane torches in a gesture of readiness.

Boo was the only one that did not know the connection between Reese, Fred, Tina and Suzie. Why Suzie and Tina did not face their fathers was a case of, 'maybe they did not see us, maybe we will get away with this, it is too late anyway'.

As far as Salami and Boo were concerned, the bikers and farmers were just as dangerous as facing Reese. There had never been a hint of respect between Reese and the boys since their first meeting. That first shift when Reese had addressed Boo, Salami, Ziggy and Frog as girls. Life working in the steel mill was a war between them, which only got worse with the injury to Ziggy and the death of Frog. Salami and Boo knew that Reese was the cause. In return Reese blamed them for his own injuries, the burn scares. Hate and revenge was on both sides of the coin.

Like John Wayne in True Grit, Salami and Boo headed directly towards the bad guys. With their torches, Tina and Suzie lit the fuses that the boys held.

Suzie hesitated. "We are not going to kill anyone are we?" A nervous excitement shook in her hands.

"No," answered Boo. "We are trying to stop them from catching us. These explosives will make big enough holes in the earth to swallow their vehicles."

"Okay, as long as no one gets hurt." Suzie lit the fuse that Boo was holding.

At the last moment, Boo and Salami turned to the outside in a wide circle. Farmers, bikers and the Jeep were grouped together in the centre. All, at the same instant, tossed their lit sticks of explosives. Vehicles dodged, swerved and ran over the smoking sticks.

Salami and Boo met behind the group. Deciding to chase after them with another barrage of fire, the boys attacked. Despite the number to sticks of explosives being tossed by everyone, the expected booms and bangs were long in coming. Organized chaos developed in the middle of a farmer's field. In every which direction, the vehicles dispersed only to attack with a new barrage of flying sticks.

Among the yelling voices, roaring engines of bikes and trucks, heads turned to each other with mouths saying, "These things must be duds."

Fred watched Reese light another fuse from the hot end of the stubby cigar. "Funny, they do not look like duds."

No sooner had the words left Fred's lips when the sticks of explosives began to explode. Sparks and light illuminating the shadows of the early evening. Balls of exploding colour at the end of flares shot into the sky. Sideways, upwards, at ground level a luster of fireworks on Canada day happening in old man Perkins' field.

A smile of colour glowed on Suzie's face as she ooed at the red, blue and greens darting across the field.

"What a show," yelled Tina, leaning out of the truck's window tossing another stick of fireworks into the air. Childish laughter sounded from Tina and Salami.

"Give them some more," encouraged Boo.

Taking her eyes from the splendid view, Suzie reached for several sticks to light at the same time. Boo's stronger arm threw them as fast as Suzie handed them to him. Without end the fireworks were exploding one after another. Trucks and bikes drove through bursts of rainbow colours. In the mayhem of speeding automobile and motorcycles traveling in scattered directions, no-one was colliding with each other.

Like chickens with their heads cut off, the bikers scrambled about the field dodging twirls of snake shaped flares. Hog and his bike were doing donuts while Speed was heading off doing a wheelie. One by one, a farmer would fall from the back of a truck like scattered tooth picks. Reese lit and tossed as many flare sticks as he was able to light. With a foot, Reese opened a second box.

A show of spectacular splendor enlightened the heavens for all to see. In a place where farms are miles apart and the majority of the fireworks were exploding close to the ground, only old man Perkins and the kids were the audience. From the comfort of the rocking chair, old man Perkins watched with a smile at the corner of his eyes. This was not what he had intended to happen to the fireworks. But by and by, it was not that bad of a show. Every once in awhile, old man Perkins noticed the bobbing of faces over in the tall grass. Heads bobbed up and down like tin targets at a carnival show. Oo's and ah's drifted through the tall brown grass.

"Hey kids!" hollered out a squeaky old voice. "I see you all hiding in the grass." Perkins motioned with a hand for them to come forward. "Come on up to the porch and sit. It is a better view from here."

First to make a move was the youngest boy who did not hear all the stories about old man Perkins. Eagerness overcame the reluctance of the others. Moments passed as the kids made their way to the front porch with a good view of the field of sparkles. Sitting close beside the old man, the kids realized that the old man was not mean at all.

Perkins had to keep the kids away until he was ready, ready to give the town and the kids a big show. Old man Perkins rocked in the oak rocking chair, with kids at his feet. All faces were aglow with wonderment. Who needs organization when a spur of the moment brings a special lasting moment.

Finally, Suzie was getting into the fun of the happening, despite the presence of her father and uncle. Tina could care less about their presence, she was having too good of a time. Lost was the danger of the men who were after Salami and Boo. Somehow the splendor of the show overshadowed the intent of the men.

Buck danced in the seat with the enjoyment of a child. Josh steered towards Boo and Suzie. Reese and Fred gained their bearings following the same direction as Boo. Voices were lost, motors fell silent under the explosions of the fireworks. In a desperate need to escape, Speed headed towards the end of the field. Bright light from exploding fireworks blinded Speed, he, his bike, Snow and Coke sailed over the fence into the pond of muddy water. Fence wire trapped the trike like a snared rabbit.

Hog's un-maned bike was heading somewhere across the field without him. Standing beside one of the farmer's trucks, Hooker starred into the eyes of a face smiling a tooth-less grin. Tires spun against the dry ground. No forward motion was gained by the truck. Hooker peered down at his bike under the front wheels of the old farm truck.

At the crown of the fence line, Fred tried to turn as sharply as the little M.G.. Unable to make the turn, the Jeep bounced up onto the ridge of stacked rocks. Like a teeter-totter, the Jeep rocked back and forth as spinning tires tried to grab at the ground. Reese dropped the spark spurting stick into the box of fireworks laying at his feet. Both Reese and Fred clambered to get free of the Jeep. As the Jeep rocked back and forth rockets of exploding balls of glamour burst into the air. Rolling down the embankment, Reese and Fred covered their heads in fear.

From the muddy pond three heads popped up above the water line. Just in time to enjoy the flash of cherry bombs exploding from the crate on the back of the trike, the three were wide eyed with wonderment.

Hooker watched in disbelief as the farmer spun the tires of the truck. There was no way the old truck would drive over Hooker's bike. The last of the passengers in the back of Josh's truck had bailed out when the twisters failed to exit the box. In moments the rest of the loose fireworks began to ignite. Leaving the truck in gear, the three riders in the front seat bailed out. Buck sat up from the ground smiling at the sight of the truck. Bursts of light rocketed skyward while the truck slowly crawled into the distance.

Removing a red liquorice from smacking lips, one that a young friend had given to him, old man Perkins said in a soft voice. "Best damn fireworks I have seen in this town in sixty years."

Eyes of happy kids watched the sky a burst in colour. "BEST DAMN SHOW," announced old man Perkins' new friends.

CHAPTER 10
MEMORIES IN A SONG

Once they felt that they were a safe distance down the highway, Boo and Salami turned the truck and the M.G. onto a concession road. Making several different turns in different directions, the boys felt safe enough to stop. Evening's darkness was creeping from the east horizon. Miles south, the faint bursts of fireworks was still playing in the sky. For a moment everyone sat quietly. There were no motors running, no-one speaking. A thud, thud of each one's own heartbeat could be felt. Crickets began to make their mating sounds after the initial interruptions from the truck and little car faded.

Salami crawled out of the open window to stand on the roof of the truck. "I do not see any signs of anyone following us."

Suzie brushed back tangled hair with trembling hands. "I am nervous, scarred and excited all at the same time," sighed Suzie, looking over towards Tina. "But, I think we are in big trouble."

"Yeah," agreed Tina. "Our fathers are going to kill us."

Tina sat on the door of the M.G.. "At least my car does not look as bad as my Dad's Jeep."

Trying to piece things together, Boo gazed from Tina to Suzie. Their resemblance was too close. "You two are cousins, and your father is driving the Jeep that is following us."

"Yeah," agreed Salami. "Tina told me that, that was her father." Suddenly it dawned on Salami. "Reese is also in that Jeep. He is your father." Salami pointed a finger a Suzie.

"He is," nodded Suzie, a smug look on her face. "So."

Boo jumped from the seat of the car as if he had realized that he was sitting beside the enemy. "Shit, Reese is your father. Shit, shit!"

"Reese killed one of our best friends," said Salami, sliding to a sitting position on the roof of the truck.

"I do not believe you." Tina shook her head defending Suzie's father. " When was this suppose to of happened?"

"Our friend Frog was killed at number four blast furnace. He was cremated in a molten slag pot. Reese, your father was the foreman on shift." Boo looked into Suzie's eyes with daggers of hatred. "He was after us from the first day we stepped foot into the steel mill."

In a fit of fear, Suzie escaped from the car's seat. Grabbing Tina by the arm, Suzie pulled her away from the car. "I do not believe that." Flashes of incidents passed through her mind. Facts added up. "My Dad said that someone tried to kill him. Someone put those burns on his back and neck."

Behind Boo's back the flashes of fireworks hung in the distant sky. Here, far from that enjoyment, a sense of betrayal hung in the air. The girl's eyes darted between Boo and Salami. In an instant, emotions had changed.

Suzie pointed a finger directly at Boo. "Are you the one that tried to kill my father?"

It was hard for Boo to give a truthful answer. He hated Reese, but not Suzie. No words came from Boo's mouth, he stood there silent, as the girls moved to the front of the car.

Salami and Tina caught each other's eye. A slight forgiving tilt of the head was passed between them. Under the circumstances their loyalties were not to be compromised.

"I think we should leave now," said Tina, moving across the front of her car. "Are you going to stop us?"

Boo lifted hands from the driver side door. Stepping backwards, Boo moved around the back of the car to the opposite side where the truck stood. Before the girls inched their way into the car, Boo reached onto the dash for the little white mouse.

An explanation would not change anyone's mind. It was best to let things end. As the little red M.G.'s engine roared to life, heading onto the gravel road, the girls did not give the boys the satisfaction of looking back. Salami lingered with thoughts and eyesight on the disappearing car and Tina. Turning to the open window of the truck, Boo placed the mouse and its hay bed on the truck's dashboard. It seemed easy for Boo to move on and not to linger on what-if's.

Since his early years, Boo had been alone. Making his way in life without attachments, was the norm. Thinking this way made it easier when someone got close then suddenly left. At this moment, he thought only for a brief second about Irene. Where was she at this moment?

"Boo," informed Salami. "I see lights coming this way."

"I am tired of running Salami." Boo stroked a finger over the mouse's back. "I do not care who it is. I am ready to take on those bikers, farmers or Reese," Boo's voice was mellow without hatred, he was stating a fact.

Stomping on the floor boards as he drove, Fred tried to put out the remainder of the fire. Most of the inside of the Jeep was scorched from the fireworks. All Reese was concerned about was the fact that the Jeep ran.

"Keep this thing going," urged Reese, spitting repeatedly. "I am going to put an end to this chasing. I am not going to travel all over this country after two ass-holes."

"Reese, do you think this is getting a little out of hand." Fred was beginning to have second thoughts. "I am willing to rough these guys up, just for the pleasure of a good fight, but what is your goal?"

"Goal, I will show you my goal." Reese reached around the seat to pull back a tarp. "This is my goal. To use this to get rid of a pain that has haunted me from the first day I laid my eyes on those four girls."

"Girls?" Fred repeated, looking back behind the seat.

"I got rid of one of them for good, up in smoke. Frog is encased in slag for eternity. One guy named Ziggy, is out of commission for a good long time." Reese spat out the last of a cigar that he had chewed to shreds. "Now with a little help, Salami and Boo are going to join their friends."

Fred's eyes widened in disbelief. A good fight was one thing, but to use weapons to hurt someone? Unconsciously, Fred slowed the Jeep down.

"Keep this damn thing going," yelled Reese, drawing a covered case forwards. "This is going to end, my way."

Fred's inner thoughts were not as strong as his huge stature. Reese was the leader. Somehow Fred was going to take orders regardless of how he thought. Right and wrong was not for him to decide. Reese was pulling the strings.

"Turn, I saw the lights head down that road." Reese zipped open the case on his lap.

From the moon, at eleven o'clock in the western sky, the sun's light reflected back towards earth. A dull night light illuminated the prairies. Fred wheeled the Jeep to the right just as a flash of red passed. Both Fred and Reese twisted to see the silhouettes of their daughters.

"They had their hands on our daughters," barked Reese.

Fighting with the awkwardness of the jeep, Fred fought with self thoughts about Reese, his daughter and his own conscience. "We do not know that."

"I know that." Reese laid the weapon across his lap. "They are up ahead on this road."

Boo opened the truck's door and sat on the edge of the seat. With a gentle hand, he lifted the mouse into an open palm. Unafraid, the little fellow nibbled on a hay seed held between pink paws.

Keeping watch from the roof, Salami eyed the road up and down. "Someone is coming. I see one headlight, and I know the sound of a Jeep."

"I guess it is show time. Are you ready for a fight Salami?" Boo turned the truck key ignition on and pushed in a tape of his own self penned music.

As the music grew louder, Salami flexed arms and clenched fists. Boo heard the Jeep getting closer. Just as Boo stood, reaching an arm to put the mouse on the dash all hell broke loose. Reese stood leaning over the window of the Jeep as Fred slammed on the brakes and changed gears. Stalling with a backfire the Jeep rocked to a stop. A blast of powder sent pellets towards Salami and Boo.

Time to think was not an option. Salami slid from the truck as pellets from a shotgun pinged against the metal of the truck. Boo rolled along the side of the truck still holding onto the little mouse. Fighting back against Reese and a shotgun was useless. Fleeing seemed to be a natural way of saving one's life. Side by side, Boo and Salami raced into the fresh smelling wheat. Thick stocks of wheat stems, waist high, fought the boys in their escape.

Recoiling from the blast, Fred jumped from the Jeep as Reese pumped another shell into the barrel of the shotgun. Terror filled Fred's eyes, his hands shook nervously at his sides. Fred yelled, "You can not kill them Reese. You cannot shoot them down in cold blood."

"The fuck, I will!"

Reese aimed over the hood of the truck at the shadows running in the field. A blast from the shotgun silenced the crickets, little birds scattered to the heavens. Salami and Boo dropped to the ground. Wet muddy ground from a marshy area of the field seeped into their clothes.

Boo could hear the hard breaths from Salami a short distance away. Tall cat tails and sharp blade grass hid them from sight. If Reese came after them, this marsh would not protect them.

"Boo," whispered Salami.

Boo quickly answered back, "I am fine, you?"

"So far."

Reluctantly, Fred followed Reese into the field. Fred constantly looked over shoulders, looking for signs of followers. Reese held the shotgun shoulder height and cocked, aimed downward into the wheat.

"I know you are there laying in the grass, praying for a miracle, but it is of no use. You cannot stay still forever." Black saliva dripped at the corners of Reese's mouth. "When you make a move, I will get you," said Reese, a finger tensing on the trigger of the pump action shotgun.

Boo lifted his head off of the ground. "You always needed someone or something to back you up. You are not man enough to face me one on one," Boo's voice cracked.

"I want you to pay, you bastards! No one is going to make a fool of me and get away with it. I am here to haunt you."

"Run Salami!" yelled Boo, getting up to run himself.

"This is for me," Reese's voice faded under the rapid explosions of the shotgun. A quick hand pumped new shells into the chamber of the shotgun and was fired again.

A scream of pain traversed the field. Flesh ripped easily when hundreds of pellets penetrated Salami's side. Blood and mud mixed together as Salami fell limply to the marshy ground.

"Salami," Boo's voice was apologetic, as he dropped to the side of Salami.

"I do not want to die." Salami squirmed about, his right hand trying to hold his insides in. "It is not bad, is it?" Tears glistened under the light reflected from a full moon.

A tear formed at the corner of Boo's eye. With a hand under Salami's arm, Boo tried to lift him. "It is not bad, you can make it, try."

Thinking that it would take Reese time to reload the shotgun, Boo tried to lift Salami for another attempt at running.

"This is for putting your filthy hands on my daughter."

Again, Reese's words were swallowed by the explosions from the shotgun. Before the sound reached the boys' ears, the ripping of flesh was felt. From deep within Boo a scream chilled Fred to a stand still. Salami and Boo fell heavily where they stood. Little rivers of blood formed in the mud. Millions of needles tickled Boo's legs, he felt a numbness building below his waist. Boo thought he was getting up. Opening a hand, Boo watched the little white mouse test a step onto the mud. Slowly it decided to step across the patches of wet mud.

"Natives on the war path, Boo step on it, let's go," spoken words were eerie sounds coming from Salami's dry voice.

Hands pulled at the roots of the grass. Boo pulled himself forward an inch at a time. Boo thought of the mouse, wondering if it would be okay in life. After all, life is hard to live through. Turning his head to look up, Boo marveled at the haze of light cresting through the top ends of the grass. Shadows of Reese and Fred weaved across the beams of light cast from the Jeep's headlight.

"My wife. I have a wife and son," Salami called out. "Boo, I have a son you know," Salami's agonizing voice trailed into a whisper.

Again, the sounds of relentless pain, there was a silence in the air. Cool wet mud soothed a still face as it slowly sank into the earth. All of the events over the past couple of months, even the past year, seemed forgotten. A mouse small and innocent wandered through the tall green grass. Boo wondered if it was able to get away from the pursuers. A reflecting headlight from a distant Jeep glimmered against the far evergreen trees.

"Do not forget who is the foreman and who is the subordinate worker," echoed the voice of Boo and Salami's tormentor.

Boo thought only of the mouse. At a time like this, and under such circumstances, why was he thinking of something as unimportant as a little mouse.

"Reese, there is a car stopped on the bridge," Fred nervously yelled to his partner. "On the highway, on the bridge, by those far trees."

An arched bridge spanned a lazy river that overlooked the field where Boo and Salami lay still and silent. With its motor idling, the car's bright headlights reflected against the silver painted girders of the bridge where it had stopped. Steel I-beams and channels, no doubt, cast and fabricated at All Steel in Steeltown. A home town that Boo and Salami had left behind, somehow wanting to forget, wanting to leave in memories. Even memories sometimes are best forgotten.

"Let's get out of here . . ., now!" winced Fred.

Reese opened the slip case and placed the companion of destruction into its resting place then zipped the cover closed. Reese and Fred hurried to depart.

In the distance, the Jeep's gears ground themselves because of a loose clutch plate. Boo rested quietly while listening to the engine fade into the calm of early evening. Against the soft mud, Boo's finger began to tap to the rhythm of music that could be heard coming from the truck's tape deck. Distant thoughts began to filter through his mind, thoughts of Salami's mother's broken English, the farmer's daughter, Irene. Passionate memories came back. Ziggy, his leg missing and a mind that was wasted, the short life of Frog.

Those Buddy Holly glasses that Frog wore, he was a nerd, somehow, Boo liked him and at times truly missed his presence. Music echoed in the air across the field, music that Boo had recorded when he and a band played at the Old Empire Hotel. There in the west end of town, the rough and down trodden end of town where life seemed real.

Straining to hear the words, Boo attempted to raise an ear. Those words . . ., those words . . ., he had penned, words of his own life, he had lived them, they now had become true to life.

> We raised us some hell.
> Stories and tales we tell.
> Sowing life's wild oats.
> Over trophies we gloat.
>
> Never regret the lives led.
> Life's burdens cast and shed.
> We raised us some hell.
> Stories and tales we tell.
>
> I see us not feeble and old.
> In youth stubborn and bold.
> Life cut short, not long.
> Memories are in my song.

Memories of one's life are remembered at the oddest of times. If only the chance to create new . . ..

THE END

OTHER TITLES AVAILABLE FROM
MOOSE ENTERPRISE BOOK AND THEATRE PLAY PUBLISHING
Visit our web site at www.moosehidebooks.com for complete title listings.

NOVELS
- Steeltown
- Steeltown Blues
- Roosevelt Street
- Executor of Mercy
- A Print of a Man
- Sky Flyers
- Assault of a Princess
- Assault
- Basement Bargain Price Leafs For Sale
- Five Star Investigations
- Rusty Butt (Treasure of the Ocean Mist)
- Arrow Boy
- Big Bobby Boom (and the Marble Mayhem)
- The Sidewalk
- Time Warriors
- The Letter
- Reflection
- Guilt in Accession
- Déjà vu

www.ingramcontent.com/pod-product-compliance
Lightning Source LLC
Chambersburg PA
CBHW051757040426
42446CB00007B/417